A SKETCH
OF THE INDO-EUROPEAN
FINITE VERB

NEW YORK UNIVERSITY
DEPARTMENT OF CLASSICS
MONOGRAPHS ON MEDITERRANEAN ANTIQUITY

A SKETCH OF THE INDO-EUROPEAN FINITE VERB

BY

J. A. KERNS
New York University

AND

BENJAMIN SCHWARTZ
Lincoln University

LEIDEN
E. J. BRILL
1972

ISBN 90 04 03547 8

PRINTED IN THE NETHERLANDS

TABLE OF CONTENTS

INTRODUCTION

This sketch is intended for graduate students and others interested in acquiring an over-all perspective of the IE finite verb as quickly and directly as possible. Since we endorse the concept that Anatolian departed from PIE earlier than the other IE continuants, it will be obvious that we adhere, in the main, to Sturtevant's Indo-Hittite hypothesis. A preliminary reading of the major text can be followed by an examination of the several appendices in whatever order meets the reader's interests or requirements. Our summaries are drawn from many excellent sources not always acknowledged in the text. Few, if any, of our explanations are original; the reader will realize that explanations in historical linguistics are largely conjecture, and that often one guess is as good as another. Any such which prove glaringly wrong are probably our own. More or less isolated aberrant forms, like Skt. m.p. fut. pl. I *aśnuviṣyāmahe* (which Whitney calls 'monstrous'), can be picked up in texts and vernacular usage in all languages, but the beginner can safely ignore them, interesting as they often are as straws showing which way the wind may be beginning to blow. Our selection of materials, presentation, and methodology, we hope, will meet with constructive criticisms from readers, and we shall gratefully accept whatever is brought to our attention.

J. A. Kerns, New York University

Benjamin Schwartz, Lincoln University

LANGUAGE ABBREVIATIONS

(Note: bracketed forms used elsewhere but not in this text)

A	Anatolian
Alb.	Albanian
Arm.	Armenian
[AS]	Anglo-Saxon, see OE
Att.	Attic Greek
Av.	Avestic
Balt.	Baltic
Celt.	Celtic
[Ch. Sl.]	Church Slavonic, see OCS
Dor.	Doric Greek
ET	East Tocharian
Gk.	Greek (Att. unless otherwise noted)
Gmc.	Germanic
Goth.	Gothic
HH	Hieroglyphic Hittite
Hit.	Hittite
Hom.	Homeric Greek
IE	Indo-European
IH	Indo-Hittite
Ion.	Ionic Greek
Lat.	Latin
Lith.	Lithuanian
Luw.	Luwian
M	Middle
MHG	Middle High German
MIr.	Middle Irish
MW	Middle Welsh
N	New
O	Old
OCS	Old Church Slavic
OE	Old English
OHG	Old High German
[OIc.]	Old Icelandic, see ON
ON	Old Norse
Osc.	Oscan
OW	Old Welsh
P	Pre-, Proto-
PIE	Proto-Indo-European
PIH	Proto-Indo-Hittite
Skt.	Sanskrit
Slav.	Slavic
Toch. A	see ET
Toch. B	see WT
Umb.	Umbrian
Ved.	Vedic Sanskrit
W	Welsh
WT	West Tocharian

Other abbreviations and symbols

act.	active
aor.	aorist
athem.	athematic
C	consonant; classical
dep.	deponent
du.	dual
fut.	future
G	grammeme
impf.	imperfective
ind.	indicative
inf.	infinitive
inj.	injunctive
ipf.	imperfect
ipv.	imperative
L	lexeme
loc.	locative
maj.	major
med.	medial, middle
min.	minor
m.p.	mediopassive
obl.	oblique
opt.	optative
pf.	perfect
pfv.	perfective
ph.	phase
pl.	plural
plpf.	pluperfect
p.p.	past participle
prs.	present
prt.	preterite
ptc.	participle
pvb.	preverb
redup.	reduplicated, reduplicating
sb.	substantive
sbj.	subjunctive
sg.	singular
SL	sub-lexeme
them.	thematic
V	vowel
vb.	verb, verbal
*	theoretical, unattested
>	becoming, became
<	from, came from
/	alternating with
:	in comparison or contrast with

1. Stems and endings. The traditional analysis of most IE finite verb forms is 'stem' + 'ending', always in that order. The stem contains at least the root/base/lexeme,[1] the ending at least an indication of person (or impersonality) of the subject, number, and voice, as sg. 1 Hit. *es-mi*, Skt. *ás-mi*, OLith. *ẽs-mi* 'I am'; sg. 3 Hit. *es-zi*, Skt. *ás-ti*, OLith. *ẽs-t*(*i*) 'he/she/it is'; act. sg. 3 IE **lei̯q^{u}e-ti* 'he leaves', **u̯ē-ti* 'he blows', **dō-ti* 'he gives' (some paradigmatic forms have zero endings, as Hit., Lat. *es* 'be thou'). A stem may also contain one or more characterizations or sub-lexemes, primarily qualifying the basic lexical meaning, though frequently in a way no longer determinable, as redupl. **di-dō-ti* : **dō-ti*; infix **liŋq^{u}é-* : **liq^{u}é-*/**léi̯q^{u}e-*; suffix Skt. *vā́-ya-ti* : *vā́-ti*, with intraparadigmatic accentual and ablaut variation. The stem may also contain one or more grammemes, expressing a specific grammatical limitation of tense or mood. Thus in a verbal complex consisting of S + E, the S can consist of L, or L + SL, or L + G, or L + SL + G, not necessarily in these orders. Distinctions of (a) tense are implemented by (1) ablaut and other variations in the stem, as Gk. prs. λείπε- : aor. -λιπε-; (2) presence or absence of tense grammemes in the stem, as Gk. prs. λύε- : aor. λυσ-; (3) the use of augment, see immediately below; (4) selective use of endings, as Skt. prs. sg. 3 *-ti* : ipf. *-t*; and (b) distinctions of mood by: (1) the presence or absence of a grammeme in the stem, as Skt. prs. ind. sg. *as-* : opt. *s-yā-*; (2) ablaut variation in the stem, as Gk. morphological pf. sg. 1 οἶδ-α : *ϝιδ- (> pl. 1 ἴσμεν) : sbj. sg. 1 εἴδ-ω, Skt. pf. sg. *véd-*, (pl. *vid-*) : opt. *vidyā́-*; (3) selective use of endings, as Skt. prs. ind. sg. 3 *ás-ti* : ipv. *ás-tu*. Often the total implementation of tense and/or mood involves the use of more than one of these means. In contrast, the implementation of voice is fairly stable, and prevailingly expressed by the selective use of endings, as Skt. act. sg. 3 *bhára-ti* : med. *bhára-te*, Lat. act. *vehi-t* : pass. *vehi-tur*; in Sanskrit and Greek, however, some passive categories are distinguished by stem grammemes rather than by selection of endings.

Homonyms apart, as Lat. *amāre*,[2] all IE verb forms are either non-finite or finite. Non-finite forms (verbal nouns and adjectives) name, describe, or allude to actions or states without intrinsically asserting them, and can be grammatically limited in terms of tense, voice, and sometimes number, as Lat. prs. inf. *esse* 'to be', past inf. *fuisse* 'to have been', prs. act. ptc. pl. *agentēs* '(they) doing'; and sometimes also by gender, as Lat. p.p. pl. fem. *actae*. Finite forms assert or question, etc., an action or state, and must imply person (or impersonality) of the subject and the mood, as well as tense, voice, and number (but not gender, except in periphrastic forms), as **es-ti* > Lat. *es-t*, Goth. *is-t*, etc. Both stem and ending may consist of a single morpheme, as (L) ipv. sg. 2 **es*, or of more than one, as

[1] By lexeme we mean a morpheme with specific lexical value, e.g., Eng. *wrest* : the sub-lexeme *-le* in *wrestle*, which qualifies the meaning lexically but not grammatically. In *wrest-ed* and *wrestl-ed* an element is added which furnishes a grammatical limitation (a grammeme), here of tense. The IE verb can be analyzed in terms of lexemes, sub-lexemes, and grammemes; thus, *wrest-ed* is L + G, while *wrestl-ed* is L + SL + G.

[2] Pass. prs. sg. 2 but also prs. act. inf.

(L + SL) Lat. stem *e(d)-sc-* 'feed', Hit. *at-sk-* 'eat'; med. ending (G) sg. 3 Hit., Skt. *-ta*, Gk. -το, but (G + G) Hit. m.p. sg. 3 *-ta-ri*, Lat. *-tu-r*. Various morphemes sometimes precede the stem, as augment and other inflectional prefixes [1] and preverbs [2] when functioning grammatically.

2. Simple stems. Single morphemes are of various structural types, common ones being **es-* 'be', **ei̯-* 'go', **dhē-* 'put', **dō-* 'give', **stā-* 'stand', **preḱ-* 'beg, ask', **u̯oi̯d-* 'know', **lei̯qᵘ-* 'leave', etc. All have at least quantitative ablaut variants (**s-*, **i-*, **dhə-*, **də-*, **stə-*, **pr̥ḱ-*, **u̯id-*, **liqᵘ-*, etc.,) variously distributed and often non-ablaut variants (e.g., **léi̯qᵘe-*) as well.

3. Characterized stems. These (L + one or more SL) may have (1) reduplication, in several varieties, as full reduplication in Hit. *lahlahh-* 'fight repeatedly', or reduplication of an initial sound, as in **le-loi̯qᵘ-*, **di-dō*; infixes, nasal, as **li-ŋ-qᵘe-* (probably recast from earlier **li-ne qᵘe-*) and perhaps others; (3) suffixes, in many varieties, as **-sḱe-*, **-i̯e-* in **pr̥ḱ-sḱe- : preḱ-*, **u̯ē-i̯e- : *u̯ē-*.[3] As for reduplication, it is convenient, even if psychologically unsound, to treat all such morphemes in IE verbal morphology as formants. In origin they are probably symbolic 'clippings' of the first member of a repeated word sequence. Beside the full reduplication mentioned above there are many shorter varieties consisting of consonant + vowel (CV) and vowel + vowel; in the CV types the particular vowel was presumably earlier dictated by that of the following syllable, but in early IE proper [4] certain reduplicating vowels had come to be largely grammaticalized for use in particular categories, as (prevailingly) *-e-* in athematic presents and all perfects, and (again prevailingly) *-i-* in thematic presents. Later changes of various sorts somewhat confuse this pattern (for discussion of athematics, thematics and perfects, see **4**, **5**, and **16** below).

4. Athematic stems and their inflection. The general PIE accentual pattern of certain important categories (e.g., active present indicative) was accented stem in sg. 1, 2, 3 : accented ending in du. and pl. 1, 2, 3. With stem internal vocalism corresponding to this accentual pattern, all stems of the type discussed in **2** above were 'biphasal', having full-grade vocalism ('major phase'), **és-* before sg. endings, but reduced or zero grade ('minor phase'), as **ъs-* or **s-* before du. or pl. endings. All the quantitative ablaut variants (**s-*, **i-*, etc.,) in **2** are minor phases thus paradigmatically distributed with the corresponding major phases (**és-*, **éi̯-*, etc.,). Now, during one period at least, the most common form of the act. prs. pl. 3 ending was (postconsonantally) *-ént*, hence pl. 3 **s-ént*, **i̯-ént*, **liqᵘ-ént*, etc. The frequency of such forms as **liqᵘént* led to the emergence of a neological sg. 3 **liqᵘé-t* beside older **léi̯qᵘ-t*, leading eventually to a complete paradigm built on monophasal **liqᵘé-*, really an embryonic thematic of type B (Brugmann's desig-

[1] Cf. Toch. *p-* imperative, as EWT ipv. sg. 2 *p-yām* ,make.'

[2] Sometimes later incorporated within the stem, as OIr. *ro-* which converts a preterite into a specific perfect, e.g., *·cechain* 'sang', but *roichan* 'has sung', with reduplication phonologically disguised.

[3] For fuller listing and discussion of stems, esp. present stems, cf. Brugmann KVG pp. 494-537; Hirt IG, vol. iv, pp. 192-239; Meillet, Intro.[1] pp. 197-226; also **13** below.

[4] By IE proper we mean the period after the separation of Anatolian from PIE.

nation), needing only the qualitative ablaut change of stem-final *-e-* to *-o-* at certain points in the paradigm to make it a quite recognizable thematic 'injunctive' of type B. The popularity of this new pattern was enhanced by the apparently increasing use of the suffixal formants *-sḱe-*, *-i̯e-*, etc., (whatever their functions may have been); as newly added and once meaningful morphemes they very probably took the word accent at their first appearance, so that e.g., not only would pl. 3 **tr̥pi̯é-nt* be thus accented, but also sg. 3 **terpi̯é-t* > **tr̥pi̯é-t*, even without assistance from analogy. As uncharacterized thematics are rare or non-existent in Hittite, while the *-sḱe-* and *-i̯e-* characterized thematics are fairly common, we may surmise that in the long run these characterizations did more to increase the popularity of the now emerging thematic pattern than did the purely analogical forms of other persons evoked by the athematic ending pl. 3 *-ént* in uncharacterized stems. In IE proper, both simple and characterized thematics became common.[1]

5. Thematics and their IE proper proliferation. During the emergence of Anatolian, the thematic type was becoming popular in incipient IE proper, so that old biphasal **léiqᵘ-/*liqᵘ-́* developed a thematic competitor **liqᵘé-* (Brugmann's type B), with stem final accented *-é-* in imitation of stems ending in such formants as *-sḱe-* and *-i̯e-*, as well as the analogical development described immediately above. It is questionable whether any simple stems of this type occur in Anatolian at all. In IE proper competition between the newer type **liqᵘé-*, now fairly frequent, and the older maj. ph. athematic **léi̯qᵘ-* produced a conflation **léi̯qᵘe-* (Brugmann's type A), the youngest and most popular type in late IE proper.[2] The absence of this uncharacterized thematic type in Hittite and its wide prevalence in IE proper constitutes an isogloss between the two.

6. Half thematics. A stem type with formant *-i̯e-* in certain persons (esp. sg. 1 and pl. 3), but with stem-final *-ī-*, *-ĭ-* (both ill understood, but possibly the result of contraction) in other persons, has been called 'half thematic' and is readily observable in Italic, Baltic, Slavic, and possibly Germanic.[3] This may also be connected with dissyllabic heavy bases [4] in *-ē(i̯)-*.

7. *h* and *m* endings; emergence of the IE proper perfect. Two series of personal endings demand our attention at the outset: (1) The '*h*' series with sg. endings somewhat variously restored, but yielding ultimately Hit. prs. sg. 1 *-hi*, sg. 2 *-ti*, sg. 3 *-i*, IE proper pf. sg. 1 *-a*, sg. 2 *-tha*, sg. 3 *-e*; the plural endings are generally the same as those of the '*m*' series discussed immediately below; (2) The '*m*' series with PIE sg. 1 *-m*, sg. 2 *-s*, sg. 3

[1] Hittite possibly preserves an earlier stage of ablaut reduction in such forms as pl. 3 *as-anzi* (: sg. 3 *es-zi*) with partial retention of the old stem internal vocalism in contrast to its complete loss in IE proper, as Skt. *s-ánti*, Lat. *s-unt*. But it is also possible that an analogically restored major phase, as in pl. 1 and 2 of some verbs of this type (pl. 1 *epweni*, pl. 2 *epteni*), but pl. 3 *appanzi, asanzi* has become *a-* by a Hittite '*a* umlaut' before *-nzi*.

[2] Note fading of quantitative ablaut.

[3] It is doubtful whether stem final *-ī-* (written *-ei-*) of Goth. sg. 2 *sōkei-s*, sg. 3, pl. 2 *sōkei-þ* is inherited as such from IE, or arose by contraction within Germanic.

[4] Hirt's term, still quite generally in use; a verb base ending in a long vowel or long diphthong in its normal grade. But even in the normal grade the second element of the diphthong often disappears under conditions unknown.

-t, pl. 1 *-u̯e/-me*,[1] pl. 2 *-te*, pl. 3 *-nt* [2] (plurals probably with ablaut variation [3]). In Hittite some active presents are formed with the *h* series, others with the *m* series, but in IE proper the *h* series is restricted to the perfect, a functional tense category completely unattested in Hittite, hence the PIE functional distinction between the two series cannot have been one of tense. The assumption that forms with *h* endings are intrinsically stative, those with *m* endings intrinsically active, is scarcely demonstrable (cf. unquestionably stative sg. 1 Hit. *es-mi*, Skt. *ás-mi* 'am'; unquestionably active Hit. *tehhi* 'put'), see also **16** below. For PIE it is better to assume that the *h* series is merely older. But as certain IE proper derivative categories (optative, subjunctive, pluperfect indicative) arose, it was invariably the newer *m* series that was used even in forms based upon perfect indicatives with original *h* type endings, as Skt. pf. opt. sg. 1 *ri-ric-yā́-m* : pf. ind. *ri-réc-a*.

8. Injunctives; secondary and primary endings. It is likely that, at the outset, forms with *m* series endings could have had any shade of meaning that would later emerge morphologically and functionally in distinct categories of tense and mood. Morphologically unchanged survivals of these multifunctional forms are the so-called injunctives. One of the earliest derivative categories was that of specific indicative presents. This was implemented by the addition of a deictic *-i* ('here and now') to four of the *m* endings, *-m, -s, -t, -(e)nt*,[4] the so-called primary endings. The corresponding unextended endings, while still retaining some degree of their old multifunctionality, came increasingly to be used with preterital meaning (by relegation, of course), the so-called secondary endings. In Hittite this apportionment was rigorously carried out. In IE proper, while the apportionment of 'primary' and 'secondary' endings was in general of the same nature, yet in some of the dialects 'secondary' endings regularly occur in some present forms, e.g., Dor. sg. 2 φέρε-ς, Lat. *vehi-s*,[5] Lith. *vẽža*, and most strikingly the OIr. conjunct presents, as sg. 3 **bhere-t* > *·beir* (which has lost *-t*, not *-ti*); all such forms are almost certainly retentions, not innovations. Meanwhile pl. 1 *-u̯e/ -me*, pl. 2 *-te* were not directly or immediately involved in the primary-secondary dichotomy; both could have permissible extensions in *-s* and *-m* (whose original functions we do not know), so that e.g., *-me, -mes, -mem* were substantially free variants. This could be and in part was exploited for functional reassignment, e.g., Skt. neo-primary *-mas* (with occasional supererogatory Ved. *-masi*), and the morphologically dissimilar pl. 2 *-tha* (perhaps after a pf. sg. 2 ending!), neo-secondary *-ta* by relegation. Hittite also achieved a neological primary-secondary distinction for these persons, but in a still different way; the extended forms *-we-m/-me-m, -te-m*, after *-m* had become *-n*, developed analogical neo-primary *-wen-i/-men-i, -ten-i*, leaving *-wen/-men, -ten* as neo-secondary by relegation.

[1] Cause of *u̯/m* alternation unclear, possibly phonological (PIE *-u̯* after *u-* > *-m*?); in any event, with functional redistribution in IE proper, as *u̯-* dual and *m-* plural.

[2] Sometimes *-ent* after a stem final consonant.

[3] Except pl. 2 *-te*.

[4] But apparently not in the corresponding *h* endings. Up to this point we have treated *-mi, -si, -ti, -(e)nti* as unitary morphemes, but it should now be clear that in origin these are binary morpheme sequences.

[5] Usually explained as loss of final *-i* from a primary ending, but the contrast of noun sg. loc. **u̯eghes-i* > inf. *vehere* is striking.

9. Certain *m* endings. The medial endings sg. 2 *-so,* sg. 3 *-to*, pl. 3 *-nto* (and 'primary' *-soi̯, -toi̯, -ntoi̯*?) are obviously somehow related to the active endings just discussed, cf. the table below.

'Active'	'Medial'
-s	-so
-t	-to
-nt	-nto

It is unclear whether the forms in the second column are extensions of those in the first, or the first reductions of those in the second. In any event, the implementation of different voices seems to have evolved from a unitary morphological situation.

10. The verbal dual. Since no duals have been found in Anatolian, the entire dual category is to be regarded as an IE proper innovation.

11. Tenses and tense systems. Out of our earlier undifferentiated injunctive there have now emerged two indicative tenses for the *m* conjugation, except for the ambiguities of the pl. 1 and 2 (see immediately above), with the creation of neo-primary and neo-secondary endings in some of the continuant languages.

12. Present and preterite; IE proper differentiation into imperfect and aorist. Exclusive reliance on personal endings to distinguish between present and preterite was sometimes evaded in our oldest IE proper dialects by augment (prefixal **e-*), so that e.g., sg. 2 *léi̯q*^{u}*e-si* was necessarily present, **é-lei̯q*^{u}*e-s* necessarily preterite, while injunctive **léi̯q*^{u}*e-s* (older than either of the others) could be either present or preterite, as Dor. sg. 2 φέρε-ς. Augment does not occur in many of the later attested IE proper dialects, but most of these have a neological imperfect indicative category of obviously monodialectal origin,[1] which may have replaced an earlier augmented category.

The co-existence of simple stems and many characterized stems of the same verb, as also of B and A thematics (Brugmann's labels) brought about a welter of morphologically distinct present stems. Hittite sets up a full paradigm (present, past) for each, retaining fairly consistently the specific functional meaning of the characterization. In IE proper the functions of these characterizations became blurred, the newer in each dialect retaining only a stylistically colorful quality as against the older simple stems; so, too, the younger A thematics as against the older B. IE proper exploited this situation by retaining the preterites but not, as a rule, the presents of the older types for dry, factual statement, but both the present and the preterite of the newer more colorful stems. Hence, in sharp contrast to Hittite, one and the same paradigm exhibits a wide variety of characterized present stems for any one verb, though the selection, viewed in retrospect, appears rather random. No one verb preserves the same characterized present stem in all the continuant

[1] Sometimes coalesced periphrastic as Lat. *tacē-ba-m,* Goth. wk. prt. *þahai-da,* Lith. *mily-davau* (otherwise Stang), OCS *vezě-achъ*. Sometimes suppletively used optative forms, as WT *yem* 'I went', Arm. *ei* 'I was' < **es-ī-m*.

dialects, nor does any one language use the same characterization in all its presents, e.g., simple athematic **ĝheu̯-* 'pour, sacrifice', (isolated Ved. sg. 2 *hó-ṣi*), redupl. **ĝhe-ĝheu̯-* recast in Skt. *ju-hó-ti* 'sacrifices', thematic A **ĝhéu̯e-* in Gk. χέ(ϝ)-ω 'pour', characterized **ĝheu̯-de-* in Goth. *giu-tan* 'pour', doubly characterized **ĝhu-n-de-* in Lat. *fu-n-dō*. The preterite of these presents are IE proper 'imperfects', whereas preterites to older stems whose presents had fallen out of use are IE proper 'aorists'. This aorist category, accidental as its origins were, grew in popularity until the stylistic advantages of its contrast with the imperfect made it desirable to form aorists even where no alternative stems were available for such apportionment. Thus various forms, morphologically quite unlike these root aorists, arose to fill the need. We now see two archcategories, the present and aorist tense systems, the latter more fully diagnosed in **20** below. So far, we have discussed the former in two sub-categories, the present and imperfect indicative; the latter in only one, the aorist indicative. Broadly, our two archcategories are mutually unpredictable, the genesis of the ultimate chaos of IE 'principal parts.' Provisionally, IE proper came to have three (or four) archcategories or tense systems: present, aorist, perfect, and future, insofar as the last was a tense category.

13. Present stem types. Here follows a rough listing of the chief structural types of 'present stems', athematic and thematic, simple and characterized, that occur in Hittite and IE proper; in Hittite some of these athematic types occur with *h* endings, and some with both *h* and *m* endings. Athematics are given first in their major phase, then (after a slash) in their minor. Accentually, most thematic classes, whether simple or characterized, can be subdivided into Brugmann's groups A (accent on a pre-stem final syllable) and B (accent on stem final). The latter is unquestionably the older (see **5** above), but eventually A becomes much more common both in recastings, as **gʷm̥sḱé-ti* > pre-Skt. **gacchá-ti* > *gáccha-ti* and in new formations, as **rḗ-dhe-* > Goth. inf. *rēda-n* : athem. *rē-* in Lat. dep. sg. 3 *rē-tur*. If in certain classes no B forms are attested, it can be presumed that the whole class is a late formation. There are, of course, many later shifts of accent, some in individual cases, some systemic in particular languages, and there are many later formations which postdate the period when ablaut operated automatically and hence do not conform to its principles. As for characterized stems, the ideal way of proving that a suspected formant is truly such, is to cite an etymologically related form from the same or another language that does not contain it, though the mere occurrence of a fair number of etymologically unrelated stems of some length but closely parallel in phonetic structure may arouse a strong suspicion that we are dealing with a formant. To save space we do not cite comparison stems here, but indicate a formant by printing it in **bold-face**; in the study of an individual word or stem, a brief search of specialized historical grammars and etymological dictionaries will usually prove that a formant is or is not involved. Indeed, since we do not know the history of PIE back to its beginnings, there is often a chance that some phoneme contained in a stem that we regard as simple may originally have been a formant. We number our structural types somewhat arbitrarily and avowedly not chronologically, but in what we hope is a fairly systematic way. Those interested in relative chronology will bear in mind that athem. 1 is the oldest of all, and that 9B and 15B are the oldest thematics.

Athematics

1. *és-/s⊥, éi̯-/i⊥, dhḗ-/dhə⊥, dṓ-/də⊥, stā́-/stə⊥*. Historically monosyllabic, and probably once the most numerous class, with some of the oldest verbs belonging to it. Surprisingly, perhaps, this type became belatedly productive in OLith., where some thematics seem to have developed by-forms recast in this athematic pattern, as e.g., sg. 1 *liek-mì* : usual *liek-ù*. A similar situation may have existed in Tocharian.

2. Dissyllabic base, theoretically ending in *-ē-*, *-ō-*, *-ā-*, or *-ēi̯-*, *-ēu̯-*, etc. Two sub-types: (a) Maj. ph. accent on first syllable, **réu̯dē-* > maj. ph. **réu̯də-*(as Skt. sg. 3 *ródi-ti*), min. ph. **rud(ə)⊥* (Skt. pl. 1 *rudi-mas*, pl. 3 *rud-ánti*), and **mléu̯ēi̯-* > maj. ph. **mléu̯əi̯-* > **mléu̯ī-* (Skt. sg. 3 *brávī-ti*), min. ph. **mleu̯(əi̯)⊥* > Skt. pl. 1 *brū-más*, pl. 3 *bruv-ánti*; (b) Maj. ph. accent on second syllable, **ĝenṓ-* > **ĝnṓ-*, the accentuation suggesting that the long vowel of the second syllable was earlier a formant, added to simple stems of type 1. Note also that (a) such major phases frequently pervaded the whole paradigm, so that there was no minor phase, and (b) the theoretical vocalism of the first syllable was sometimes analogically restored, or replaced by a surrogate, and that such major phases also could come to be monophasally used.

3. Reduplicated, as ***dhédhē-*** / *-ə⊥*. Despite the accent on the reduplication, the second syllable of the major phase retains the *-ē-* on the analogy of type 1 *dhē-*. Both the redupl. vowel (IE *-e-* > Skt. *-a-*) and that of the min. ph. (IE *-ə-* > Skt. *-i-* or zero) are subject to analogical alteration in Greek, etc.

4. *i̯un**ég**- / i̯ung⊥*.

5. *qᵘr̥**nā́**- / **-nə⊥***.

6. *str̥**néu**- / **-nu⊥***. In types 5 and 6 the formant, though conveniently treated as a suffix, is probably an ***-n-*** infix in a dissyllabic stem.

7. *u̯**és**-*. Minor phase only attested (no active forms); accent and ablaut unexplained (Skt. med. sg. 3 *vás-te*); ***-s-*** shown to be a formant by the Lat. cognates sg. 1 *ex-uō, ind-uō*, etc.

Thematics

8. B *dik̂é-* in Skt. *diśá-ti*; A *déi̯k̂e-* in OLat. *deicō*, Class. Lat. *dīcō*.

9. A (only) ***gi**ĝñe-*, as in Lat. *gignō*. The *-i-* as reduplicating vowel seems normal for thematic stems.

10. B *i̯u**ŋ**gé-*, as in Skt. yuñjá-ti, Lat. *jungō*; A *i̯úŋge-* in Lith. *jenkù* (prt. *jekaũ*).

11 B. *tm̥**né**-*, in Dor. τάμνω. A in Gk. τέμνω. In this and many following thematic classes the forms show that the suffix was not added to a pre-existing simple thematic stem (as *8. *teme-*), but a monosyllabic athematic stem (as *1. *tem-*).

12 B. *pr̥k**sk̂é**-* in Skt. *pr̥cchá-ti*, PLat. **po[rc]scō* > *pōscō*; A Skt. *gáccha-ti*.

13 B. **uq**sé**-*, implied by the vocalism of Skt. *úkṣa-ti*, though the form is recast as A, as with most examples of this formant; shown to be a formant by e.g., Lat. I *voc-āre*.

14. *pek**te**-*. A forms only, as Lat. *pectō* 'comb' : Gk. πέκω id.

15. B. *ml̥**dé**-* in Skt. *mr̥ḍá-ti* : A. *mél**de**-* in Gk. μέλδω, OE *melt-an*.

16. B. *mr̥**dhé**-* in Skt. *mr̥dha-ti* : A. in Skt. *márdha-ti*.

17. B. *t̥r̥ué-* implied by vocalism of Skt. *tū́rva-ti*; for A. **gᵘéi̯ue-* cf. Lat. *vīvō*, etc.

18. B. *spr̥i̯é-* in Gk. σπαίρω, Lith *spiriù*; A. *speki̯e-* in Skt. *páśya-ti*, Lat. *spec-iō*.

Quite apart from all the specific classes in which it occurs, the thematic suffix *-i̯e* may have more than one origin. It may be partly from an old relative particle (underlying also the adj. suffix *-i̯o-* and the relative pronoun *i̯o-s*) but it may also have been abstracted from the stem final in heavy bases in *-ēi̯-*. Here begins a group of 'denominatives', noun or adjective stems extended by the formant *-i̯e-*, mostly of accentual types B, but largely of post-ablaut origin. Types 19, 20 often undergo monodialectal contraction, thus presenting a neo-athematic appearance, as 19. *-ā-*, 20. *-ē-*.

19. *-ā-i̯e-*, as in Lith. *dovanóju* < *dovanà* 'gift.'

20. *-ē-i̯e-*, as in Lat. *albeō* 'be white' < *albus*.

21. *-i-i̯e-*, as in Lat. *finiō* < *finis*, Lith *dalyjù* < *dalìs* 'share.'

22. *-u-i̯e-*, as in Gk. μεθύω < μέθυ 'honey, wine', Lat. *metuō* < *metus* 'fear.'

23. *-eu̯-i̯e-*, possibly in Gk. βασιλεύω < βασιλεύς.

24. *-C*(any cons.)*-i̯e-*, as in Gk. ὀνομαινω (< * ὀνομανi̯ω) < ὄνομα.

25. *-e-i̯e-*, as in Lith. *menù* 'think' : Lat. *moneō* 'cause to think, warn.' This type has causative or iterative function; its initial *-e-* is often the stem final of a pre-existing thematic, but could probably have been analogically extended. Where the pre-existing thematic had lexeme internal *-e*, this usually has ablaut grade *-o-*, as in the Lith. : Lat. examples above.

We also find various monodialectal characterizations, some of which never proliferated. Various compound characterizations occur, some from earliest times, as 6, 12 in Hit. *ar-***nu-ske**-; 11, 17 in Skt. *r̥*-**n̥-vá**-; 9, 12 in Gk. **γιγνωσκε**-; 10, 12, 18 (***-n-sk-i̯e-***) in Arm. *kor̃nčʻi-* (: aor. med. sg. 1 *koreay*). It is natural to suppose that every well defined characterization would originally have had a distinct function, yet at least by late IE proper times these special functions, if they ever existed, had become blurred. A single old verb often has several differently characterized stems, variously apportioned in the various languages, often more than one in a single language, without discernible functional or semantic distinction. In most instances the native Sanskrit grammarians could detect no such distinctions; for them these characterizations were only 'present stem forming elements', because generally absent in concurrent non-present stems. In the relatively few instances where the native grammarians could detect a specialized function, they termed the corresponding non-functionally specialized verb (or other word) a 'primary' (regardless of what or how many characterizations it might contain), and the specialized one a 'secondary', thus arriving at four types of secondaries, viz., denominatives (our nos. 19-24), causatives (our 25), desideratives and intensives (not included in our list). In some of the secondaries, when non-present stems were needed, they were formed by a standard extension of the present stem, thus giving Sanskrit a group of 'weak' verbs. The situation is not too dissimilar in many of the other languages.

14. Neological imperfects. Some languages have recategorized optatives (see **38** below) as imperfects, others have coalesced periphrastics.

a. *Sanskrit.* See **38**a.

b. *Latin* (and Italic generally?). Latin has a coalesced periphrastic imperfect indicative the second member of which is (in its own right) an *-ā-* aorist to stem **bheu̯ā-*, etc., i.e., **bhu̯ā-* (cf. OIr. sg. 3 *ba*, Lith. *bùvo* 'was') > Lat. sg. 1 *-ba-m*, sg. 2 *-bā-s* and the analogical pass. sg. 1 *-ba-r*, sg. 2 *-bā-re*/*-ris*, etc. The first member for conjugations II, III, IV was probably an oblique case of a verbal noun (sg. instr. in **-ē-* or **-ei̯*) ultimately assimilated to the present stem when necessary, as sg. 1 II *monē-ba-m*, III *vehē-ba-m*, OLat. IV *scī-ba-m*, Class. Lat. *sciē-ba-m*; analogically I *curā-ba-m*. For the verb *sum* an isolated *-ā-* aorist **esā-m* > Lat. *era-m* etc., serves as imperfect. The only p-Italic example is Osc. pl. 3 *fu-fa-ns* (ending phonologically = Lat. *-ba-nt*). To be sure, this solitary instance is formed, exceptionally perhaps, from the suppletive perfect stem *fu-* to prs. *sum*.

c. *Old Irish*. The paradigm is as yet unexplained, as (strong conjugation) sg. 1 *·berinn*, sg. 2 *·beirthea*, sg. 3 *·bered*, pl. 1 *·beirmis*, pl. 2 *·beirthe*, pl. 3 *·beirtis* are formed from the present stem. The sg. 3 could come from **bhere-to* (old ending not yet committed to the middle); pl. 1 and 3 could have ended in an enclitic (reflexive?) **-se*. Since the whole paradigm is followed also by deponent verbs (which in other categories have forms distinct from the active), the pl. 1 and 3 might once have had middle reflexive meaning, though in Old Irish there was no longer a semantic distinction between deponents and actives.

d. *Welsh*. Mostly recategorized optatives, see **37**d and Appendix.

e. Gothic (All Old Germanic somewhat similar). The 'weak preterite' is a controversial category. It may be a coalesced periphrastic imperfect, with its second member a root aorist of IE **dhē-*/*dhō-* 'set, do' (cf. Skt. aor. sg. 3 *á-dhā-t*) > PGoth. sg. 1 **-đō-m*, sg. 2 ** -đē-s*, sg. 3 **-đē-đ* (this apportionment of IE *e*/*o* is shown by ON *-þa*, *-þer*, *-þe*), and is obviously formed after that of IE *e*/*o* in thematic stem finals, but in the dual and plural a redupl. athem. aor. IE pl. 1 **dhedhə-me*, etc., (but with PGoth. analogical lengthening of redupl. vowel and alteration of stem final) > Goth. *-dēdum*, *-uþ*, *-un*. The first member, to which these endings are added, may have been an old verbal noun of some sort, but in the actual Gothic forms it is, in most instances, the descriptive present stem, as in sg. 1 VIII *nasi-da*, IX *salbō-da*, X *habai-da*, XI *fullnō-da* : prs. sg. 1 *nasja*, sg. 3 *salbō-þ*, *habai-þ*, *fullni-þ* (analogical for **-nō-þ*?). For the class numbers here used the terms 'Weak I, II, III, IV' are usual, these forms now occurring only in verbs with present stems as shown, though, if these forms were once imperfects, they may also have once occurred in all verbs. Those verbs not now exhibiting these forms have 'strong preterites' conflated from IE aorists and perfects (see **32**d) which have become functionally identical. If our supposed imperfects also eventually became functionally identical with these old aorist-perfect conflations, they may have died out except in verbs to which aorists and perfects had either never been formed, or were for some reason going out of use. This is in essence the theory of the 'weak preterite' held by Bopp and many of his followers, as set forth in modern dress by Kieckers, etc.; other theories have been vigorously and competently set forth by Collitz and others. So far no one theory has completely driven all others from the field.

f. *Tocharian*. Recategorized optatives, see **37** and **38**.

g. *Armenian*. See **38** for the recategorized imperfect of *em* 'am', sg. 1 *ei*, sg. 2 *eir*, sg. 3 *ēr*, pl. 1 *eakʿ*, pl. 2 *eikʿ*, pl. 3 *ein*. All other imperfects are analogical to this, so I and II identical (!) sg. 1 *berei*, etc., III *layi*, *layir*, *layr*, *layakʿ*, *layikʿ*, *layin*, IV *hełui*, *hełuir*, *hełoyr*, *hełuakʿ*, *hełuikʿ*, *hełuin*. Whether the forms of classes I-IV are entirely analogical, or coalesced periphrastics with minor phonological adjustments (as in Latin and Gothic) is open to question.

h. *Lithuanian.* Descriptively, imperfects consist of the infinitive stem + sg. 1 *-davau*, sg. 2 *-davai*, sg. 3, pl. 3 *-davo*, pl. 1 *-davome*, pl. 2 *-davote*, as *vèž-davau* 'I carried', etc. In some dialects the initial of the second member is *-l-* for *-d-* and in still others, by interdialectal conflation, *-dl-*. If this is, as often maintained, a coalesced periphrastic, we might expect its second member to be recognizably the preterite of *dė-* 'set, do', or *duo-* 'give', but the actual preterites of these verbs are *dĕjau* and *daviaũ* respectively, neither coinciding exactly with the bound forms above, though conceivably an earlier independent **davau* may have existed. Moreover, this imperfect is Lithuanian only; its absence in Latvian and Old Prussian suggests that it did not emerge immediately upon the loss of the IE type of imperfect, but that at a considerable period after the loss of that imperfect, it emerged as a specific Lithuanian neologism. Note also that it has only the iterative, not the durative function, whereas the IE imperfect and most of its neological replacements had both. This lends some support to the view of Stang[1] that all Lithuanian imperfects have been generalized from preterites to present iterative stems in *-auja-*, as prs. sg. 1 *keliáuju*, prt. *keliavaũ*, and that the *-d-* / *-l-*, *-dl-* is merely a hiatus breaker, though its need is scarcely apparent.

i. *Slavic.* A typical OCS imperfect is (to prs. sg. 1 *mьn-ǫ*, inf. *mьně-ti*) sg. 1 *mьně-achъ*, sg. 2, 3 *mьně-aše*, pl. 1 *-achomъ*, pl. 2 *-ašete*, pl. 3 *-achǫ*. It seems to be a coalesced periphrastic, the first member being an oblique case of a verbal noun in some instances related to the present stem, in others to the 'infinitive' stem (< an older aorist stem), and with its final phonologically somewhat altered or adjusted. The initial of the auxiliary is sometimes PSlav. *-*ě*- (> *-*ja*), sometimes *-*a*. The *-*ě*- might come from a lengthened grade aorist, less probably an augmented imperfect; as for *-*a*, Stang (l.c.) thinks this could come from an IE pf. (sg. 3 **ōse* not convincingly attested elsewhere, but cf. Skt. *ā́sa*); others consider *-*a* somehow analogical (so e.g., Hermann KZ 60, 1951, pp. 68 ff.). The development of IE **s* is not strictly phonological; after either PSlav. *ě*- or **a*- the **s* should have been retained as *-s*, but there are many *-s-* aorists in which *-s-* is preceded by *i-*, *u-*, *r-*, or *k-*, and in these contexts *s* would phonologically > *-ch-* at some period, regardless of the following vowel. It is clear that the auxiliary was eventually recast, and before new stem final *-e* our *-ch-* would phonologically > *-š-* ('second palatalization').

j. *Albanian.* The (Central Albanian) ipf. of sg. 1 *jam* 'am' is sg. 1 *ishja(m)*, sg. 2 *ishje*, sg. 3 *ishte*, pl. 1 *ishim*, pl. 2 *ishit*, pl. 3 *ishin*. What this form itself is, we do not know (perhaps an *-s-* aorist?). In any event the imperfects of all other verbs follow this pattern: sg. 1 *punoje*/*-ja*, *rrisje*, *prishje*, etc., with only minor phonological adjustments or alterations. Whether these are coalesced periphrastics or total neologisms or analogies is open to question.

15. The PIE *h* conjugation. The *h* conjugation, like the *m* conjugation, originally made no tense distinctions. Hittite, perhaps alone of the Anatolian languages, developed a full *h* paradigm, present and preterite, functionally parallel to the same categories of the *m* conjugation, and to a certain extent analogical morphologically. Except for sporadic instances, no Hittite verb has both *h* and *m* presents; this is presumably the PIE situation.

[1] Vgl. Gram. d. balt. spr. Oslo, 1966, p. 365.

For a present, Hittite recast the old characteristic personal endings, sg. 1 **-Ae*,[1] sg. 2 **-tAe*, sg. 3 **-Ee* on the analogy of the *m* 'primaries' *-mi*, *-si*, *-ti* as **hi*, *-ti* (the laryngeal preventing assibiliation), *-i*, whereas in IE proper these became the perfect endings *-a*, *-tha*, *-e*. For a preterite Hittite recast sg. 1 **-Ae* as *-hun* after the *m* 'secondary' *-un*. In the sg. 2 and sg. 3 Hittite made occasional use of a late PIE incipient preterital tense marker *-s-* sometimes followed by *m* secondary endings. In the sg. 2 it used the old personal ending *-ta* (< PIE **-tAe* without analogical alteration), or the tense marker could be followed by either the personal ending *-ta* or by the *m* 'secondary' ending *-s*, i.e., **-s-ta* or **-s-s* both > *-s*. In the sg. 3 Hittite used the tense marker followed by the *m* 'secondary' ending *-t*, **-s-t* > *-s*, thus falling together with one form of the sg. 2. This was enough to induce optional use of *-ta* and *-sta* as sg. 3 endings also. In some of the other Anatolian languages sg. 1 *-ha* was retained, eventually at least, as a preterite in contrast with prs. sg. 1 Luw. *-wi* (the *w* a common allophone of *m*). While on the one hand this seems to point to an Anatoloian (exclusive of Hittite) restriction of the *h* category to the preterite (superficially paralleling the IE proper restriction to the perfect), on the other hand the occurrence of Luw. prs. sg. 3 *-i* (beside the *m* form *-ti*) does not accord with such a conclusion and indicates a situation approximating that of Hittite. For lack of forms this paradoxical situation must remain unresolved.

16. The IE proper perfect. In IE proper the *h* conjugation, despite the conservatism of its endings, sank to a mere tense, the perfect (another archcategory), normally though analogically formed to most *m* conjugation presents; hence the complete paradigm of an IE proper verb includes both *m* and *h* forms. The structural differences between Hittite *-hi* conjugation stems and the IE perfect stems are: (1) Reduplication. In Hittite this is rare and when it does occur is for the most part differently structured, as *as-as-hi*, whereas consonantal reduplication with *-e-* (Gk. sg. 1 λέλοιπα, Lat. *cecidī*, Skt. *cakára*; exceptional in Hittite, as *memai*) is the norm in IE proper (except initial **i̯- *u̯-*, and, of course, vowels, where various forms occur). Unreduplicated **u̯oi̯da* (maj. ph. Skt. *ved-*, Gk. (ϝ)οιδ-, Goth. *wait*; min. ph. Skt. *vid-*, PGk. **ϝιδ-* > ἰς-, Goth. *wit-*) is exceptional; (2) Biphasality. Hittite shows traces but no clearly emerging pattern. In the IE perfect, however (to judge especially from Sanskrit, vestiges in Greek, and Germanic), the biphasality is clear, most commonly with full-grade *-o-* vocalism in the major phase, as **léloi̯qᵘ-*: zero-grade min. ph. **le-liqᵘ-´*; (3) Suffix characterizations. Some Hittite *-hi* present stems are characterized by suffixal *-na-* and *-sa-*, but there are no suffix characterizations (except later by analogy or monodialectal developments) in the IE perfect.[2] In IE proper the *h* conjugation became functionally incompatible with active presentiality, and where a one-time *h* conjugation verb needed to be expressed as an active present, it was recast with *m* endings, cf. Hit. prs. sg. 1 *tehhi* 'set, place' : IE **dhē-mi* (later **dhi-dhē-mi*, Gk. τί-θη-μι).

[1] A for *a*- coloring laryngeals, E for *e*- coloring. Non-laryngealists will, of course, consider these endings in their IE forms.

[2] Thus the PIE pre-form of Hit. prs. sg. 1 *tarnahhi* etc., develops transparently in IE proper as pf. **dedora* (cf. Skr. *dadā́ra*) : a newly minted prs. sg. 1 **dr̥nā́mi* (cf. Skt. opt. sg. 3 *dr̥ṇīyāt*), or if thematic **dr̥nō*, cf. Goth. pl. 3 *-taúrnand* (Feist, Goth. Wb. p. 12a).

17. Survival of the perfect as a category. The IE perfect survives and is both morphologically and functionally distinct in Indo-Iranian and Greek, and descriptively recognized as a category. In Q-Celtic, and to some extent in Tocharian, while still morphologically distinct in all persons, it is not conventionally recognized as a separate category, but forms part of the so-called preterite. In Latin and Germanic the IE perfect is conflated with various aorists; descriptively, the resultant joint category is the Latin 'perfect' system and a part of the Germanic 'strong preterite' system. It is lost, except vestigially, in P-Celtic, Baltic, Slavic, Armenian, and Albanian. Wherever it is considered part of a joint category (so Old Irish, Tocharian, Latin, Germanic), this is due to a functional overlapping and ultimate interchangeability with the aorist. At various times and places periphrastic perfects have arisen, even in Hittite.[1]

18. Neological perfects. Greek has two neological perfects: (1) The 'aspirated perfect.' In the perfect middle, the pl. 2 ending -(σ)θε phonologically aspirated immediately preceding π, β; κ, γ to φ; χ respectively, hence pl. 2 *τετραπ-σθε > τέτραφ-θε. Ultimately this worked back into the active paradigm of many verbs, so that to prs. τρέπω the pf. sg. 1 is no longer *τετροπα but τέτροφα etc.; (2) The *-k-* perfect. As with *-k-* aorists (see **24** below) we have to do with the enclitic addition of an asseverative particle (IE **-qe*) in the first instance to such forms as *ἔ-στα-ε-κε > ἔ-στη-κε this giving rise to sg. 1 ἔ-στη-κα, sg. 2 ἕ-στη-κας and ultimately pl. 1 ἑ-στή-καμεν etc., the new *-k-* (stem final) making its way into the whole active imperative, optative, and subjunctive paradigm. These *-k-* perfects proliferated analogically until they far outnumbered the IE type, so that native grammarians called them 'first perfects'(!) because of their sheer numerical preponderance, leaving the type λέλοιπα to be called a 'second' perfect, and τέτροφα an aspirated ('second') perfect, etc. The *-k-* perfect infiltrated the active paradigm much more successfully than the *-k-* aorist, but it never got into the middle voice, whereas such med. aor. sg. 1 forms as ἐθήκαμεν (instead of normal ἐθέμην) occur in late Greek. See also **32**.

19. Pluperfect. An IE pluperfect is sparsely attested in Sanskrit and Greek as augment + perfect stem + secondary *m* ending, e.g., Skt. sg. 1 *ájagrabh-am* (*-am* for expected *-a* < **-m̥* as almost always in Sanskrit), Hom. pl. 1 ἐ-πέπιθ-μεν; both languages show some analogical recasting. But some Sanskrit and Greek pluperfects imply a suffixal *-s-* before the personal ending, as Skt. sg. 2 *á-viveś-īs*, sg. 3 *á-viveś-īt* (with compensatory lengthening of *-i-* for loss of following *-s-*), Hom. 'augmentless' sg. 1 πε-ποίθ-εα(-εα < **-es-m̥*), Att. sg. 1 ἐ-λελοίπ-η (η by contraction < -εα). This *-s-*, even if sometimes due to late *-s-* aorist types, is ultimately due to the PIE tense marker found in the Hittite sg. 2, 3 *-hi* conjugation preterites. Other pluperfects are monodialectal, as Lat. *-eram* < **-is-ā-m* (extension of an *-s-* aorist by an *-ā-* aorist), MW *carasswn* (recasting of an *-s-* aorist after the Welsh imperfect). Periphrastic pluperfects occur widely.

20. The aorist. For the origins of the aorist as an IE proper functional category, see **12** above. From being at the outset a mere stylistic option, perhaps rather casually

[1] *turiyan harweni* 'we have harnessed.'

exercised, the aorist came to be an expected and almost mandatory functional resource of every paradigm. Morphologically, from the outset, it was variegated structurally and became ever more variegated. Broadly speaking, aorists are such either by relegation from former present-stem status as PIE preterites apparently on the way to becoming IE imperfects (but ousted by more favored rivals), or as neologisms. Over IE generally there are six formations, two of which have already been mentioned in **12** above.

21. Relegation of root aorists. Monosyllabic athematic stems as sg. 3 **é-dhē-t* 'put', **é-dō-t* 'gave', **é-ĝnō-t* 'knew', **é-stā-t* 'stood' > Skt. *á-dhā-t, á-dā-t, á-sthā-t* : Gk. ἔ-γνω-ν, ἔ-στη-ν (ἔ-θη-κα, ἔ-δω-κα by later extension); Arm. semi-isolated sg. 3 *e-d;* Lith. sg. 3 *-žin-o* (the same form without preverb is a present 'know' with neological preterite); OCS sg. 2, 3 *zna, sta* (possibly extended to an *-s-* aorist, as other persons of their paradigms clearly are, since final **-s* and **-s-s, *-t* and **-s-t* are all regularly lost); Goth. sg. 1, 3 *stōþ* (sg. 3 ending incorporated into stem, cf. pl. 3 *stōd-un*); all concurrent with variously characterized presents. Earlier biphasality has mostly been levelled out either in late IE or monodialectally, always in favor of the major phase.

22. Lengthened grade aorists. These are apparently athematic, as **sēd-* in Lat. pf. stem *sēd-* : prs. *sĕde-ō,* Goth. pl. *sēt-* : prs. *sita,* Lith. prt. sg. 3 *sė́d-o* : (recast) prs. *sė́d-u,* OCS aor. sg. 1 *sěd-ъ* (recast as thematic) : prs. *sęd-ǫ; *bhōd-* in Lat. pf. *fōd-* : prs. *fŏd-iō,* or *vād-* : prs. *vădō,* Goth. prt. *fōr* : prs. *far-a,* Lith. extended prt. *smõg-ė* : prs. *smag-iù,* Alb. aor. sg. 1 *mol-a, fol-a* (stem internal *-o-* < IE *-ē-*) : prs. *mjel, flas.* These perhaps follow asymmetrically the models **é-dhē-t, *é-dō-t, *é-stā-t.* In some cases a stem internal *-ē-* is not a lengthened grade, but the normal grade of an original IE long, while the concurrent present may have the reduced grade *-ə-*, so e.g., Lat. pf. *frēg-* : prs. *frang-ō.* In Latin such an *-ē-* is often analogically imitated, as pf. *ēg-, cēp-* for expected **āg-, *cāp-* : prs. *ăg, căp-,* cf. the Germanic strong preterites ON *ōk,* Goth. *hōf.*

23. Athematic aorists in -ē-, -ā-. Some of these are by relegation, many are analogical: **é-mьnē-t* > Gk. 'second aorist'[1] passive ἐ-μάνη-ν; **bheu̯ā-* in Lith. prt. sg. 3 *bùv-o; *bhu̯ā-* contracted in OIr. prt. sg. 3 *bá/ba* (also as incorporated auxiliary in Lat. sg. 1 *-ba-m,* Osc. pl. 3 *-fa-ns*). Presents from such stems, though perhaps once common, are ill attested in the earlier languages, but some vestiges imply biphasality, as e.g., Skt. sg. 3 *brávī-ti, ródi-ti, vámi-ti* : pl. 3 *bruv-ánti, rud-ánti, vam-anti* (type **13**, 2). Later analogical presents of this type (some of them contracted from characterized stems in *-ē(i̯)-i̯e-, -ā-i̯e-* and so only apparently athematic, as Lat. sg. 2 *cupī-s, amā-s,* OIr. sg. 3 *·móra,* Goth. sg. 3 *habai-þ, salbō-þ,* Lith. sg. 3 *sák-o* are monophasal major phase, as are also the aorists themselves). The majority of the attested forms are analogical, with quasi-suffixal *-ē(i̯)-* and *-ā-*, so Lat. isolated imperfect(!) **es-ā-m* > *er-am* after **bhu̯ā-m,* most strikingly so in Baltic, where all other types of aorists have been thus recast, as **liqᵘe-* to **liqᵘā-,* Lith. sg. 3 *lìk-o; *sqābh-,* a lengthened grade aorist, cf. Lat. pf. *scāb-ī* : prs. *scăb-ō,* Goth. prt.

[1] Conventional Greek grammar describes a more numerous morphological type as 'first', and a less numerous type of identical function as 'second', regardless of chronology. All Greek aorists so far discussed are, in fact, 'second' aorists; the newer aorist types, the more numerous, are the 'firsts.'

skōf : prs. sg. 1 *skab-a*; *sqābh-ē-* in Lith. sg. 3 *skõb-ė* : prs. *skab-iù*; in PSlavic and PArmenian *-ē-* and *-ā-* aorists were extended to *-s-* aorists, at least in certain persons, as OCS sg. 2, 3 in *-ě*, *-i*, *-a* (extended or unextended?) : sg. 1 *-ě-chъ*, *-i-chъ*,*-a-chъ* (*-chъ* < **-so-m*); Arm. pl. 3 *lkʿi-n*, pass *lkʿan* might < **liqᵘē-nt*, **liqᵘā-nt*, but sg. 1 *lkʿi* cannot < **liqᵘē-m*, it must have been somehow extended. The Armenian functional apportionment of *-ē-* and *-ā-* aorists as active and passive respectively is perhaps incipiently paralleled in Baltic, where the *-ē-* preterites belong mostly to transitive verbs, the *-ā-* preterites to intransitives or intransitive-inchoatives. Finally, dissyllabic *-ē-* and *-ā-* stems structurally identical with these figure as subjunctives in some languages; the identity may be functional, since as injunctives they could have had 'modal' (non-indicative) as well as preterite indicative value.

24. Indo-Iranian aorist passives in -*i*. The absence of normally inflected dissyllabic active and middle aorists in *-ē-* and *-ā-* in Indo-Iranian is noteworthy, as against their occurrence in Greek, Armenian, Slavic and Baltic. It is possible, however, that the sg. 3 passive aorists in *-i* are endingless forms with stem-final **-ə* > *-i*, otherwise variously explained. Many of these are, of course, analogical. For an endingless med. sg. 3, cf. Hit. *esa*, *kesa* : *esa-ri*, *kesa-ri*.

25. The -*k*- aorist. In Greek, athematic root aorists which maintain a distinct minor phase in the dual and plural, e.g., pl. 1 ἔ-θε-μεν, ἔ-δο-μεν, ε-ἷ-μεν extend their major phase in the singular by *-k-*, ἔ-θη-κα, ἔ-δω-κα, ἧ-κα with analogical personal endings. The Latin 'perfect' stems *fēc-*, *iēc-* are almost certainly identical with Gk. -θηκ-, -ηκ- but with generalization of the *-k-* throughout the active paradigm in all Italic, e.g., Lat. prs. *fac-iō*, *iac-iō*, Osc. prs. sbj. *fak-iiad*.—If Phrygian sg. 3 αδ-δακε-τ/-τορ is a cognate, and present, it shows an even wider (med. prs.) generalization of *-k-*.[1]

26. Relegation of thematics. Root thematic stems, mostly of type B, as sg. 3 **é-liqᵘe-t* (< **liqᵘé-t*) > Skt. *á-rica-t*, Gk. ἔ-λιπο-ν and (with various monodialectal conflations, extensions, etc.) Lat. pf. *fid-ī* 'split' (or perfect with loss of reduplication), Goth. prt. pl. 1 *bit-um*, **lihv-um* > *laihv-um* (conflation), Lith. sg. 3 *lìk-o* (extended to an *-ā-* aorist), all concurrent with a present either of thematic type A or variously characterized. There are a few such aorists of type A beside characterized presents, as Skt. *á-sada-t* : prs. *sī́da-ti* (disguised reduplication); Gk. ἔ-τεκο-ν : prs. τίκτ-ω; a few monosyllabic stems, as Skt. *á-hva-t* : prs. *hváya-ti*, Gk. ἔ-σχο-ν : prs. (σ)ἔχ-ω reduplicated stems [2] as Skt. *á-rīrica-t* (causative, probably a monodialectal functional shift), **é-u̯eu̯(e)qre-t* > Skt. *á-voca-t*, Gk. sg. 3 **ἐ-ϝεϝεπο-ν* > εἶπο-ν (reduplication proved by subjunctive εἴπ-ω etc.), Hom. ἔ-πεφνο-ν: prs. θείν-ω, ἤγαγο-ν : ἄγ-ω, ἤραρο-ν : ἀραρ-ίσκω; Arm. sg. 3 *arar* : sg. 1 *aṙne-m*. There are sporadic later instances of such relegation in several dialects where old preteritally used injunctives or imperfects of IE type have been replaced by neological imperfects, as

[1] This extension is also responsible for the Greek 'first perfect' (active only, but in all persons), and possibly for the *-k-* extension in the Lith. imperative (asseverative particle **qe-*?).

[2] There are more of these than might be expected. Earlier redupl. them. prs. **gᵘhigᵘhne/o-* > Ved. prs. *jíghna-te*, but the one-time present stem underlying Hom. aor. ἔ-πεφνο-ν seems to have been ousted in pre-Greek by prs. **gᵘheni̯e-* > θείνω.

(possibly) Lat. 'perfect' *lamb-*, OCS aor. sg. 2, 3 *nese* : prs. sg. 3 *nese-t*, Arm. aor. sg. 3 *e-ber* : prs. sg. 1 *bere-m*.

27. The -*s*- aorists. The tense marker -*s*- often seen in the Hittite sg. 2, 3 *h* preterite and vestigially in some IE pluperfects is the model for all varieties of the -*s*- aorists, although here it occurs in all persons and numbers. These aorists must have been first created either (1) as reinforcement of existing lengthened grade aorists, or (2) in cases where no obsolescent present stems were available (cf. **12** end) for relegation, but became so popular in many dialects [1] that they were set up even where older aorists were already in use. With new coinages, particularly denominative verbs (especially those formed with -*i̯e*- suffix as -*ā-i̯e*- etc., and with frequent contraction to -*ā*-, so as to superficially resemble athematics), the -*s* aorists were almost *de rigeur*.

28. The simple -*s*- aorist. Whether or not automatic ablaut was still operative in late IE proper, simple -*s*- aorists occasionally show biphasality in Sanskrit. In cases of reinforcement of older aorists, as described immediately above, this is just a continuation; in neologisms it may well be analogical. Except for a pl. 3 -*r* ending [2] (extended from the *h* conjugation) in some languages, *m* endings are used. Thus, major phase **u̯eĝh-s*- > **u̯ēks*- > Skt. *vākṣ*-, Lat. pf. *vēx*-, OCS *věs*- : prs. *váha-ti*, *veh-ō*, *vez-ǫ*. The minor phase, only in the Skt. middle, as act. sg. 1 *á-rauts-am* : med. *á-ruts-i*, but Gk. act. sg. 1 ἔ-δειξ-α : med. ἐ-δειξά-μην (sg. 1 *-*sm̥*, pl. 3 *-*sn̥t* > Gk. -σα with the pl. 3 analogically recast as -σαν); from these the tense marker -*s*- was analogically recast as -σα- throughout the paradigm except the act. sg. 3. In OCS the endings sg. 1, du. 1, pl. 1 became thematic -*sъ* / -*chъ*, -*sově* / -*chově*, -*somъ* / -*chomъ* and the sg. 2, 3 are always suppleted by some other aorist. In Old Irish indicatives of the simple -*s*- aorist do not survive, but injunctives do in certain persons, in a modal sense only. Descriptively these are the -*s*- subjunctives, cf. **39** below.

29. The -*əs*-/-*is*- aorist. In Sanskrit these fall together into the -*is*- aorist, sometimes analogically, as biphasal act. *á-pāviṣ*-, med. *á-paviṣ*-, but monophasal act. and med. *á-bodhiṣ*-. From *-*əs*-, *ĝēr-əs*- comes Gk. ἐ-γήρα-σα (the -σ- retained analogically after e.g., ἔ-δειξ-α), OCS sg. 1 *nes-ochъ* reformed from prs. *nes-ǫ* (whether the -*o*- < IE -*ə*- is disputed). From *-*is* comes Lat. pf. sg. 2 *vīd-is*(*tī*), cf. Skt. *a-ved-īt* < **a-ved-ist*. The paradigm of this Latin word, and possibly some others, was conflated with forms going back to **u̯oi̯d*- and the *vīd-is*- forms of the sg. 2, pl. 2, and in part of the pl. 3 gave rise to an extension in -*is*- in these persons in all 'perfect' stems regardless of their origin, e.g., *cecid*-, *fēc*-, *vēx*-, etc., to *cecid-is*-, *fēc-is*-, *vēx-is*- and such derived categories as the indicative pluperfect and future perfect, subjunctive perfect and pluperfect, and the perfect active infinitive.

[1] But not in Germanic or Baltic.

[2] This ending eventually acquired plural meaning in both Hittite and IE proper. In Hittite *h* presents used pl. 3 -*nzi*, but *h* preterites retained the -*r* ending, analogically extended to *m* preterites also. In the IE proper perfect, pl. 3 -*r* endings occur in Sanskrit, Latin, Tocharian, and (conflated with an -*nt* ending) Old Irish. In Sanskrit this ending is extended to athematic aorists (including -*s*- aorists) and sporadically in athematic imperfects.

30. Thematic *-se-/-o* aorists. These occur in Sanskrit as *-sa-* in sg. 1 *á-dik-ṣa-m* (here *-am* < **-om*, cf. sg. 2 *á-dik-ṣa-s*), Gk. act. sg. 3 ἔ-δειξ-ε, OCS active only sg. 1, du. 1, pl. 1 *-ъ*, *-o-vě*, *-o-mъ*, and perhaps also Lat. *vēx-it*, but other explanations have been advanced. Certain persons of the OIr. *-s-* subjunctive are thematic.

31. Neological aorists. Any such category, if it forms a subdivision of a larger monodialectal category conflating IE perfects and aorists (so Latin, Old Irish, Tocharian, and possibly Albanian) is treated in **32**. Armenian has a neological aorist not forming part of such a conflated category. Its most characteristic morpheme is IE **-sk(e)-* > Arm. *-ç-* (common enough over IE generally as a sub-lexeme, a present-stem characterization, type in **13**, 12), but used as a grammeme (tense marker) only in Armenian and partly in Tocharian, see **32** e. This is sometimes added to a form resembling the present stem, as in sg. 1 *la-çi* to prs. *la-m* and sometimes to an old *-ā-* suffixal aorist stem, as sg. 1 *asa-çi* to prs. *as-em*. But most commonly in the case of verbs with presents of conj. I, this grammeme is added to an earlier sequence **-isā-* (**-is-* aorist stem + an *-ā-* suffixal aorist?). An **-is-ā* sequence occurs also in the Latin pluperfect indicative, but is added to the 'perfect' stem, as sg. 2 *vēn-erā-s*; **-is-ā* > PArm. **-ea-* (so still in sg. 3 *-ea-ç*) but syncopated to *-e-* in other persons. Finally, the inflection completely follows that of the 'strong' *-ē-* suffixal aorist (including substitution of an *-ā-* suffixal aor. in the pl. 1) in the active. Thus:

sg. 1	laçi	asaçi	sireçi	but	lçi
2	laçer	asaçer	sireçer		lçer
3	(e)-laç	asaç	sireaç		(e)-liç
pl. 1	laçakʿ	asaçakʿ	sireçakʿ		lçikʿ
2	laçēkʿ, -ikʿ	asaçēkʿ, -ikʿ	sireçēkʿ, -ikʿ		lçēkʿ, -ikʿ
3	laçin	asaçin	sireçin		lçin
: prs.	sg. 1 lam	asem	sirem		lnum

32. Monodialectal categories conflating the IE perfect and aorist. A functional falling together has already taken place in CSkt. (though not in Vedic) but the morphological categories remain distinct. Broadly speaking, this is also true for Old Irish and Tocharian, but here the grammarians lump the two together solely on functional grounds as preterites, whereas in Latin and Germanic there is much morphological conflation as well, though on wholly different lines. The resulting neo-categories are the Latin 'perfect' and the Germanic 'strong preterite.'

a. *Latin.* Note first that no phase distinctions survive in paradigms where such would have existed in IE. There are four (or five) types: (1) Originally reduplicated stems, mostly old perfect stems, as **stest-* > *stet-*, OLat. *memord-* > CLat. *momord-*, IE **ĝheĝhoud-* (with loss of reduplication, as always when the major phase survives) > Lat. *fūd-*, **tetag-* (but this might be an IE redupl. aorist, cf. Hom. τεταγών not *τεταγώς) > *tetig-*, *peper-* (*re-pper-* haplological loss of redupl. vowel) concurrent with present stems in sg. 1 I *stō*, II *mordeō*, IIIa *fundō*, IIIb *pariō*, IV *re-periō*. Under various conditions the reduplicating vowel has been shifted (incipient but never very successful anticipatory vowel harmony), as *momord-*, *didic-* : prs. *di(c)scō*, *tutud-* : prs. *tundō*, or the reduplication has been lost, especially in preverbal compounds with later spread to the simplex verb, or the lexeme vowel has been shifted for various causes, in the end becoming sometimes the old major or minor phase, sometimes following the present-stem vocalism, as *popōsc-* (prs. **pr̥kskō* > **porcscō* > *pōscō*); (2) IE lengthened grade aorists, as **sēd-*, **ēg-* (perhaps analogical for earlier **ōg-*, cf. ON *ók*), *cēp-*, *vēn-*, **bhū-* > **fū-* > *fu-* (shortening before following vowel) to prs. II *sedeō*, IIIa *ago*, IIIb *capiō*, IV *veniō*, *sum* (suppletive); (3) IE *-s-* aorists, as *māns-*, *vēx-* (quantity hidden but probable), *spēx-*, **hauss-* > *haus-* to prs. II *maneō*, IIIa *vehō*, IIIb *-spiciō*, IV *hauriō*; (4) Analogical *-u-*, *-v-* 'suffixal' type, the 'suffix' abstracted from type (2) *fu-* and generally modeled after the present stem, as *secu-*, *monu-*, *genu-*, *rapu-*, *salu-* to prs. I *secō*, II *moneō*, IIIa *gignō*, IIIb *rapiō*, IV *saliō* and *cūrāv-*, *flēv-*, *strāv-*, *cupīv-*, *audīv-* to prs. I *cūrō*, II *fleō*, IIIa *sternō*, IIIb *cupiō*, IV *audiō*; of these *genu-*, *strāv-* have been modeled after some other stem. Occasional conflation of types occurs, as (3, 4 immediately above) **metsu-* > *messu-* to prs. IIIa *metō*. Finally, all types have beside them an extended form in *-i-*, generalized from IE minor phase **stestə-* in the pl. 1 and another in *-is-* (probably from *-is-* aorists, see **29**), as *stet-is-*, *sēd-is-*, *māns-is-*, *secu-is-*, etc., occurring in the pf. sg. 2, pl. 2 (and partly pl. 3) and all derivative neo-categories. The most drastic conflations are in the endings, which must be treated here, even out of logical context. Thus sg. 1 **-ai* (IE pf. med.) > *-ī*, sg. 2 *(-is-)ti* (latter part analogically recast from IE pf. sg. 2 **-tha*), sg. 3 *(-i-)t* (*-i-* < IE pf. sg. 3 **-e* extended by usual Lat. *-t*, or < thematic aorist *-e-t* if such once existed in Latin), pl. 1 *(-i-)mus*, pl. 2 *(-is-)tis*, pl. 3 in three forms: *-ēre* (from the IE perfect ending, cf. Hit. *-er*, Skt. *-ur* etc., though the initial *-ē-* is unclear); **-iso-nt* (thematicized *-is-* extension) > rare CLat. *-erunt* (apparently persisting in Vulg.Lat., cf. Ital. *fecero*); *-ērunt* (conflation of the other two, the usual CLat. ending). No passives are formed from any perfect stems.

b. *P-Italic.* The category is probably a conflation as in Latin, and generally called 'perfect.' Cited forms are few, though their types are bewilderingly numerous, and sometimes restricted to derivative neo-categories, some of which are differently formed from their Latin functional equivalents: (1) IE redupl. pf. in sg. 3 Osc. *dede-d*, Umb. *dede*; (2) Thematic aorists (by relegation). Osc. sg. 3 *-bene-d* (cf. Skt. aor. *á-gama-t*); (3) Lengthened grade aorist. Osc. pf. sbj. sg. 3 **hēp-* > *hipi-d*:; (4) *-s-* aorists. None are cited as perfect indicatives, but the ipf. sbj. Osc. sg. 3 *fusid* (= Lat. *foret*) seems to imply the type; (5) The *'f'* perfect. This is a neological coalesced periphrastic with thematically recast auxiliary aorist **bhu̯o-m*, **bhu̯e-s*, etc., as in Osc. sg. 3 *aikda-fe-d*, pl. 3 *fu-fe-ns*; (6) Neological *-tt-* perfect. Osc. sg. 3 *prúfa-tte-d*, pl. 3 *prúfa-tte-ns* is unclear; (7, 8) Neological **-l-* and **-nki-* forms.These are coalesced periphrastics with a participle and an adjective (?) attested only in Umbrian derivative categories, as fut. pf. sg. 3 *entelust*, *purdinsìust* and are unclear. Finally, it should be noted that at least some p-Italic perfect stems could form a passive with an *-r* ending; at least one of these, Osc. *esuf lamatir* 'let him (have been = be) beaten'(?)

c. Old Irish. Exept as noted, only 'conjunctive' preterites and 'absolute' presents (**42**) are cited. (1) From IE perfects. Normally with *-e-* reduplication and the major phase generalized, as sg. 3 *·beb(a)e*, *·bob(a)ig*, *·cechuin*, *·cech(a)ing*, *·cechlaid*, *·leblaing*, *·memaid*, *·nenaisc* (extension of *-sk-* formant from present stem), *·rer(a)ig*, *·teth(a)ig* : prs. sg. 3

(conjunct) *·bá, bongid, canid, cingid, cla(i)did, lingid, ma(i)did, nasc(a)id,* (conjunct) *·rig, tongid.* In the pl. 3 *cechnatar* etc., the ending *-(a)tar* is a conflation of IE secondary *-nt* and the perfect *-r*; the pl. 1 ending in *cechnammar* etc., has taken over this added *-r* from the pl. 3; (2) From IE lengthened grade aorists, as **u̯ēde-t > fíd, *tōke-t > taích* (: prs. *fedid, techid*), these also have pl. 1 *-ammar*, pl. 3 *-(a)tar* analogically; (3) From IE *-s-* aorists. Here we must distinguish between all those of the original *-s-* types which occurred in pre-Irish only as modally used injunctives and were eventually recategorized as the *-s-* subjunctive (**38**) and a later type somewhat analogically recast from present stems. In this type *-s-* was always preceded by a vowel and was itself doubled to *-ss-* (cf. Hom. ἐδάμασσα), the stem final becoming thematic except in the sg. 3. The sg. 3 **-(a)sst* is always phonologically lost in Old Irish, as *·mor*, but pl. 1 *·morsam*, pl. 3 *·morsat* have not been influenced by the endings of type (1) above; (4) Neological *-t-* preterites. The starting point is a very archaic athematic preterite (**13**, 1), IE **bher-t*, cf. Lat. prs. *fert*, Ved. Skt. *bharti*, apparently used in pre-Irish by relegation as an aorist, with analogical extension of *-t-* as a tense marker to other persons, as pl. 1 *·bertammar*, pl. 3 *bertar, -tatar* following type (1); a few other verbs also form *-t-* preterites.

d. *Gothic* (and in part Old Germanic generally). (1) IE redupl. perfects (redupl. vowel *-e-* > Goth. *-aí-* before *-r, -h, -ƕ*, then generalized) occur without conflation in Class VII (for Gothic verb classes cf. Appendix). All of these come from IE 'heavy bases'; those of VII. 1 have sg. lexeme vocalism **-ōi̯-*, pl. **-əi̯-*, both > Goth. *-ai-*, hence sg. 1, 3 *haíhait*, pl. 3 *haíhait-un* : prs. sg. 1 *haita* (here *-ai* < IE **-əi̯-*). The IE *-r* ending is lost in Germanic and is suppleted by aorist ending *-nt > -un*, similarly in VII 2, 3. In the remaining subclasses of VII the two phase vocalisms would not fall together phonologically, but the major phase is analogically generalized, as in VII 5 *laílōt, laílōtun*; (2) In Class VI the lengthened grade aorist occurs without conflation with perfects, and there is generalization of the major phase, as in *sōk, sōkun* : prs. *saka*; (3) In Classes I-III PGmc. had a redupl. perfect with phase distinctions intact, approximately **gegraiþ, *gegriþun*, but also a simple thematic aorist **griþ, *griþan*. The identity of lexeme vowel and near identity of ending caused all the perfect forms to lose reduplication, but the athematic ending pl. 3 *-un* (perfect) drove out thematic (aorist) *-an*. Apart from these changes there was an unexplained preference for the perfect, hence ultimately Goth. sg. 1, 3 *graiþ* : pl. 3 *griþun* : prs. *greiþa*, the first form of the preterite stem occurring in all singular forms, the second in all dual and plural forms. Classes II, III behaved similarly; (4) Classes IV and V. The bases involved were monophthongal; the pf. sg. 1, 3 would have been e.g., pre-Goth. sg. **bebar*, pl. **bebrun* (to prs. **baira*), with complete absence of lexeme internal vowel in the perfect plural, as would also have been the case with a thematic zero grade aorist. There was also, however, a lengthened grade aorist (whether as yet thematicized is not clear), with stem **bēr-* throughout. These forms were altered and reapportioned as in I-III, giving Goth. sg. 1, 3 *bar*, pl. 3 *bērun*, so also in Class V, cf. Appendix for fuller tabulation, and note that in all other Old Germanic languages, though there are vestiges of the reduplicated perfect of Class VII, it is the lengthened grade aorist which gives the normal preterite. No passives are formed from any preterite stems.

e. *West Tocharian.* Some preterite forms evolved from IE reduplicated perfects (and reduplicated aorists?), others from lengthened grade *-ā-* or *-ē-* suffixal or *-s-* aorists; still others are neological, but there is some confusion among these types. Thus the pf. pl. 3 *-r* ending has been extended to the preterites of *-s-* aorist origin as well (unlike the situation in Old Irish); also, though outside the finite categories, the perfect reduplication has been generally extended to the preterite participle of types not otherwise reduplicated. Krause-Thomas recognize six types, though because of the confusions etc., a one-to-one correspondence with the IE types is not possible. The situation is further complicated by the *fait accompli* pairing of 'primary' verbs with their respective causatives, which can involve considerable morphological dissymmetry. Examples given below are 'primary', except as noted. (1) 'Suffixless.' So KT § 432, but in § 458 they speak of stem final *-ā*, and in § 434 stem final *-i̯ā*, and compare this with Lith. prt. sg. 1 *tempiaũ*, but which we regard as involving IE stem final *-ē* : sg. 1 *kyāna-wa*, sg. 2 *kyāna-sta*, sg. 3 *kyāna*, pl. 3 *kānare* (sic!). (2) Reduplicated. Actually it is only in East Tocharian that reduplication is kept in the indicative, as sg. 3 *cacäl* : WToch. *cāla*. Schulze (who evidently believed that strong preterites of Germanic VII come from earlier reduplicated forms like those of Goth. *haíhait*, with later loss of reduplication, consequent contraction, etc.) asserted that the WToch. preterites of the same verbs had lost reduplication and undergone contraction, hence EToch. *cacäl*, WToch. *cāla*. We prefer to see IE lengthened grade aorists in these forms. (3) *-s-* aorists. sg. 1 *prek-wa*, sg. 2 *preka-sta*, sg. 3 *prek-s-a*, pl. 3 *prek-ar*; the tense marker *-s-* is retained only in the act. sg. 3, though in all persons in the corresponding middle. (4) Neological *-ṣṣ-* type (not related to the *-s-* aorists). sg. 3 *wināṣṣa*, pl. 3 *wināṣṣare*, apparently with IE *-sk-* as tense grammeme, cf. the Armenian *-ç-* aorists (**31**). (5) Neological *-ñ(ñ)-* type. sg. 1 *w(e)ñā-wa*, sg. 2 *w(e)ñā-sta*, sg. 3 *weña*, pl. 1 *weñā-m*, pl. 2 *wñā-s* (sic!), pl. 3 *w(e)ñā-re*; there are also *-ññ-* present stems. (6) Vestigial thematic type. KT suggest that the endingless sg. 3 continues either IE perfect *-e* or thematic aorist *-e-t*.

f. *Albanian*. There are two types: (1) 'Regular', as Conj. I sg. 1 *punova*, sg. 2 *punove*, sg. 3 *punoi*, pl. 1 *punumë*, pl. 2 *punutë*, pl. 3 *pununë*; Conj. II *rrita, rrite, rriti, rritëm, rritët, rritën*; Conj. III *prisha* (the *-sh-* is part of the lexeme, cf. prs. sg. *prish*), *prishe*, etc., (as in Conj. II). We know nothing of the origin of these forms; the Conj. I *-ova* etc., was earlier regarded as a loan form based on Latin Conj. I ipf. sg. 1 *-ā-bam* (!), etc. Although Albanian contains many Vulg. Latin and Romance loan words, it seems highly improbable that *-ova* is a loan form. (2) *-s-* aorists. sg. 1 *dhashë*, sg. 2 *dhe*, sg. 3 *dha*, pl. 1 *dhamë*, pl. 2 *dhatë*, pl. 3 *dhanë* (suppletive to prs. sg. *ap* 'give'). There are only a few such aorists; the *-sh-* supposedly representing IE *-s-* occurs only in the sg. 1, and we know nothing of the origin of the sg. 2 through pl. 3 endings.

33. The future. As in the case of some other mood-tense categories, the absence of a formal future in Hittite virtually proves the absence of this category in PIE. In IE proper, or at least in many of its dialects, a formal future containing an *-s-* grammeme was developed. This is best continued in Indo-Iranian, Greek, and Baltic, cf. sg. 1 Skt. *dasyā́-mi*, Gk. δώσω (Dor. δωσέω), Lith. *dúos-iu* : prs. *dádā-mi*, δίδω-μι *dúo-mi*, though the formations are not quite identical. Sanskrit has thematic **-si̯e-/-si̯o-*, Greek thematic **-se-/-so-* (but Doric **-sei̯e-*, if not of later analogical origin), Lithuanian half-thematic **-si̯o- / -si-* (perhaps a later development < **-sei̯e-* as in Doric). Vestigial forms belonging here are OLat. sg. 1 *capsō, dixō, faxō*; apparently regular in P-Italic, cf. Osc. sg. 3 *fust* 'will be' < **fuse-t*,

Umb. pl. 3 *furent* < **fuso-nt,* isolated Umb. sg. 2 *heries* 'thou shalt want' < *-*ses*; OCS fut. ptc. *byšę* (without corresponding indicative) < **bhusi̯ont-* 'about to be.' Moreover, some Old Irish verbs have an *-s-* future, generally reduplicated and inflected like an *-s-* subjunctive (closely resembling Sanskrit desideratives), cf. sg. 3 *gigis* : prs. *guidid 'asks.'* Other types of futures in various languages are specialized subjunctives or neologisms.

34. Origins of the *-s-* future. Two interrelated problems arise: is the *-s-* future related to (1) the *-s-* aorist? or (2) to the Sanskrit desiderative of type *dítsati* 'wants to give'? If (1) is true, the relationship is probably to be traced through the subjunctive of the *-s-* aorist, the conventional view; all subjunctives could have future meaning among others. And as the earliest *-s-* aorist indicatives were athematic, their subjunctives would be thematic (see **39**). The Old Irish quasi-subjunctive inflection of its *-s-* futures possibly favors both (1) and (2). Once the *-s-* future emerged as a distinct category it was formed freely even where there was no *-s-* aorist antecedent, and the stem internal ablaut (though normally full grade in Sanskrit) might follow any convenient model, often that of the present indicative. When this future category needed desiderative connotation, the form could be reduplicated, which led to the emergence of still another category, the desiderative, as in Indo-Iranian. To further distinguish the unreduplicated non-desiderative future from this, its formant might be extended to *-sei̯e-* and *-si̯e.* In sharp contrast, the Old Irish reduplicated category nearly drove out the unreduplicated but lost its desiderative connotation, and the *-se-* form was not extended. In the other dialects there are few, if any, traces of the reduplicated forms, or of desiderative connotations (except Hom. διδώσω?), though reduplicated forms may well have once existed.

35. Monodialectal and neological futures. The isolated Greek futures ἔδομαι, πίομαι, Lat. *erō* are old thematic present subjunctives implying athematic present indicatives **edmi* (cf. Skt. *ádmi*), **pīmi,* **esmi* historically replaced by Gk. ἐσθίω, πίνω, Lat. *sum.* Q̰-Italic has some functionally specialized *-ē-* subjunctives, see **39**c, namely those whose corresponding presents are the Latin III and IV conjugations. Other Latin futures are coalesced periphrastics made from a verbal noun in some oblique case and the *-*e*- subjunctive IE **bhu̯ō,* **bhu̯es,* etc., with possible affinities to Q̰-Celtic,[1] but not to P-Italic or P-Celtic. The verbal noun postulated was assimilated to the present stem of the verb, so that the Latin future is never an archcategory, but part of the present stem system. In Late PSlavic presents inherited < IE were gradually sorted out into two functional categories, the imperfective and perfective aspects. There is no clear-cut morphological distinction, though many of the perfectives had a preverb. Perfective 'presents' are functionally futures implying completion. When this is not desired a periphrastic is used consisting of an auxiliary and an imperfective infinitive. Germanic either uses the present with future meaning from context (as does Hittite), or a periphrasis consisting of an auxiliary and the infinitive. Since Germanic most probably never had an IE proper

[1] Some Old Irish futures have a stem suffix *-f-* which Thurneysen (Grammar of Old Irish, Dublin 1946, § 637) derives on severely phonological grounds < *-*su̯*-, cf. fut. sg. 3 *leic-f-id* 'he will leave' : prs. sg. 3 *leic-id,* but which has been otherwise equated with the Latin *-b-* < *-*bh*-. P-Celtic has vestiges of a future with suffix *-h-* < *-*s.*

derived subjunctive, it could never develop a future comparable to those languages which did inherit that mood. Tocharian has no future but, depending on context, both the present and the subjunctive can function as a future. Armenian uses its aorist subjunctive, itself neological, as a future. Albanian uses periphrases consisting of *do* 'will' + *-të-* + subjunctive, or auxiliary *kam* 'have' + particle *-me-* + past ptc. functioning as infinitive. Sanskrit has a neological 'imperfect' future, as sg. 3 *á-bhariṣya-t* 'he was about to carry', later often 'he would carry', hence called 'conditional' in classical Sanskrit.

36. Moods. Apart from endingless forms, bare stems widely used as ipv. sg. 2, but also vestigially in Hit. med. sg. 3 and perhaps elsewhere, earliest PIE had only one 'mood', the 'injunctive.' In later PIE this was partly differentiated into an indicative and an imperative by the selective use of endings, with the stem remaining the same in both these moods, save for the possible distribution of major and minor phases in athematics. The *i* extension added to sg. 1, 2, 3, pl. 3 *m* endings (but never the *h* endings) stressed not only presentiality ('here and now') but also asserted actuality. Thus such forms as **es-ti* and **lei̯qᵘe-ti* are necessarily both present and indicative, whereas the older injunctive **lei̯qᵘe-t*, though it could have this meaning, could have other meanings, indicative as well as modal (non-indicative). An *-u* extension applicable to the sg. 3 and pl. 3 had specifically imperative function, as **es-t-u* 'let him be', continued in Hit. *es-tu*, Skt. *ás-tu*. Here we have incipient indicatives and imperatives as morphological mood categories in seeming contradistinction to the older injunctives **es-t*, **lei̯qᵘe-t* from which both are derived. But the emerging paradigms were not completely symmetrical. Thus the bare stem of the verb serves everywhere as ipv. sg. 2 of thematics, but not universally of athematics, some of which form an ipv. sg. 2 in IE **-dhi*, Hit. *-t*, as Hit. *i-t* 'go', Skt. *i-hí*, Gk. ἴ-θι. The pl. 1 *-me*, pl. 2 *-te* endings never directly received either the *-i* or *-u* extensions. Thus in PIE there was no primary-secondary distinction possible in the pl. 1 and pl. 2. Neo-primaries and neo-secondaries for these endings, however, could be created in various ways, partly involving *-m* and *-s* extensions of *-m* and *-te*, see **8** above. The problem was acute only in Hittite, where forms with 'secondary' endings could only be preterite. But even where neo-secondaries were available, the ipv. pl. 2 everywhere used only the 'secondary' ending, as Hit. ipv. pl. 2 *taske-ten*, Skt. *bhára-ta*, Lat. *vehi-te* : prs. ind. Hit. *taske-teni*, Skt. *bhára-tha*, Lat. *vehi-tis*. Whereas Hittite has completely transformed the old injunctive into preterite indicative and present imperative, IE proper has preserved it fairly normally in the preterite and vestigially in (1) forms with secondary endings but present meaning, as Dor. φέρε-ς and (2) forms with modal function, as frequently in Vedic Sanskrit. Most importantly, no alteration or extension of stem (except for Toch. prefix *p-* and Lith. suffix *-k*, both monodialectal) is involved as between the indicative and imperative moods, though it will be involved in the contrast between indicative and optative, and indicative and subjunctive (the optative and subjunctive are, of course, purely IE proper innovations). Broadly speaking, IE proper allowed the formation of moods to stems of each archcategory. The one partial exception would be an injunctive to a perfect stem, since Sanskrit makes a rare perfect injunctive with 'secondary' *m* endings; evidence from other languages is lacking. The optative and subjunctive are IE proper neo-categories. It is uncertain which is older; the formation of the optative requires extension of the stem by a new morpheme whose origin is obscure; in contrast, the subjunctive is formed by a further though specifically IE proper recasting of certain old inherited injunctives.

37. The optative. If the corresponding indicative stem is a biphasal athematic, the optative extends its minor phase by **-i̯ē* in sg. 1, 2, 3 and mostly in pl. 3, and by **-ī-* in pl. 1 and pl. 2. Thus, operating with the verb **és-/s-´*, the optative stem is **s-i̯ḗ-* in the first group of forms and **s-ī-´* in the second. If the indicative stem is thematic, its form with stem final *-o-* is extended by *-i-*, as **bhero-i-*. These extended forms take secondary endings, as sg. 3 **s-i̯ē-t, *bhero-i-t,* pl. 2 **s-ī-te, *bhero-i-te,* etc., so that all optative inflections have an athematic appearance, those of the **s-i̯ē-t* : **s-ī-te* type being biphasal in their own right. Nowhere have these distributions been retained without change.

a. *Sanskrit.* In active optatives formed to athematic indicatives, Sanskrit largely generalizes the major phase of the optative grammeme, so that we have prs. opt. pl. 1 *syā́-ma,* pl. 2 *syā́-ta* for expected **sī-má, *sī-tá,* but in pl. 3 uses the *-r* ending *sy-úr*; in the middle the minor phase *-ī-* holds its own. In those formed to thematic indicatives, most persons and numbers are entirely as expected, i.e., prs. sg. 3 *bháre-t,* pl. 2 *bháre-ta,* but sg. 1 *bháre-yam,* pl. 3 *bhāre-yur* show slight analogical and phonological changes. Optatives from non-present stems are rather rare but do occur, as athem. aor. pl. 1 *bhū-yā́-ma* : aor. ind. sg. 3 *á-bhū-t*; *-s-* aorist optatives occur in the middle only, as pl. 1 *bhak-ṣī-máhi* 'may we share' : act. aor. **a-bhakst* > *á-bhāk*; thematic aor. opt. sg. 2 *vidé-s* : ind. sg. 3 *á-vida-t*; pf. opt. sg. 3 *vavr̥t-yā́-t* : pf. ind. *vavárt-a*. Classical Sanskrit has some future optatives, as sg. 3 *dhak-ṣye-t* 'may he burn' : fut. ind. *dhak-ṣya-ti.* Sanskrit also has a neo-category built almost wholly on the aorist optative, the 'precative', with a stem extension *-s-* after the mood stem (with little or no functional distinction from other optatives), as pl. 1 *bhū-yā́-s-ma* : opt. *bhū-yā́-ma* and prec. med. sg. 3 *bhak-ṣī-ṣ-tá.*

b. *Greek.* To a few athematic present indicatives the optative is a transparent continuant, as sg. 1 φαίην (analogical retention of **-i̯-*), pl. 1 φαῖμεν : ind. φημί; but the major phase of the optative marker often ousts the minor phase in the dual and plural as, pl. 1 φαίημεν beside older φαῖμεν. Sometimes the major phase of the lexeme is used throughout, as sg. 1 **es-i̯ē-m* (: Skt. *s-yā́-m*) > εἴην (the **-i̯-* here is, of course, not yet intervocalic, hence analogically φαίην etc.). Finally, many athematics follow the thematic pattern, as sg. 1 ἴ-οι-μι etc.; the by-form ἰ-οί-ην is an amusing hybrid. To thematic indicatives the optative is the expected φερ-οι- etc., by far the most usual optative pattern. From non-present stems, athematic aorists sg. 1 στα-ίη-ν, θε-ίη-ν, δο-ίη-ν etc., but from *-s-* aorists, as sg. 2 λῦ́-σαι-ς (partly recast after the thematic pattern), or its by-form λῦ́-σει-ας a hybrid perhaps implying earlier *λῡ-σι̯η-ς. Thematic λιποι- : ind. ἔ-λιπο-ν; fut. λῡσοι- : ind. λῦ́-σ-ω; perfect athematic optatives are rare, as pf. opt. sg. 1 εἰδείην : οἶδα; most perfect optatives follow the thematic pattern, as λελοιποι- : ind. λέλοιπ-α, and λελυκοι- : ind. λέλυκ-α.

c. *Latin.* The few surviving IE proper optatives are descriptively Latin subjunctives, all of them of the athematic type, as OLat. sg. 2 *s-iē-s,* pl. 2 *s-ī-tis,* this paradigm being more conservative in Old Latin than either Sanskrit or Greek, but in classical Latin the minor phase of the marker drives out the major, as sg. 2 *s-ī-s, vel-ī-s,* etc. The so-called perfect subjunctive always adds the mood marker *-ī-* to the 'perfect' stem (of whatever origin) extended by **-is-*, as sg. 2 **cecin-is-ī-s* > *cecin-er-ī-s.*

d. *Celtic*. Only p-Celtic has surviving forms, all functionally indicative imperfect.

e. *Germanic*. Beside athematic present Gothic etc. *is-t*, OHG has an optative survival ('subjunctive' in older descriptive grammars) sg. 1, 3 *s-ī*, sg. 2 *s-ī-s(t)*, which is recast in Gothic after the thematic pattern, as sg. 2 *sijai-s*. The optatives to thematic indicatives are fairly transparent, as sg. 2 Goth. *baíra-i-s*, etc. In one class, presents of weak II, the so-called optative is historically an injunctive. Non-present stems, strong preterites whether from IE aorists or perfects, show the athematic formation, as Goth. prt. sg. 2 *bēr-ei-s* (*ei* Gothic orthography for *ī*) : ind. *bar-*. It is this **-ī-* optative sign which is responsible for some stem internal umlauting in this category in some West Germanic languages.

f. *West Tocharian*. Here the older optatives to present stems with altered stem finals *-i-* and *-oy-* from various athematic types (those in *-i-* analogically followed by thematics also) have been recategorized as imperfect indicatives. Their place (athematics and thematics) has been taken by neological optatives built in the same way from subjunctive stems, some of these of comparatively recent origin.

g. *Baltic*. Vestiges of the IE optative survive in certain third person 'permissive' forms ending in *-iẽ* < **-oi̯-t*, and introduced by the particle *te*, as *te nešiẽ* 'let him (or them) carry.' This type of permissive, now at least, can be formed only from primary verbs with sg. 1 in accented *-ù*; all other verbs use instead the ind. sg. 3 with the same introductory particle, and even those in sg. 1 *-ù* may be so formed (as *te neša* for *te nešiẽ*).—Is the particle *te* related to the Albanian particle *të* used to introduce (and mark) the subjunctive?

h. *Slavic*. All surviving forms are descriptively imperatives, as sg. 3 *ber-i* < **ber-oi-s*, **ber-oi-t*, but pl. 2 *ber-ě-te* < **ber-oi-te*, strictly phonological.

i. *Albanian*. It is tempting to see some vestige of the IE optative in the subjunctive forms of the verb 'to be' as sg. 1 *je-më*, sg. 2 *je-shë*, etc., although this would involve the PAlb. use of primary endings, since the secondary **-m*, **-s*, **-t* would have been lost in final position.

38. The optative as imperfect. In a number of languages IE optatives have been recategorized as imperfect indicatives, or have at least influenced the imperfect forms. Thus, the Skt. them. med. ipf. du. 2 and 3 have stem final *-e-*, as *á-bhar-e-thām*, *-tām* (and even analogical prs. *bhar-e-the*, *-te*) for expected **a-bhara-* etc., while the corresponding forms of the optative, where *bhar-e-* would have been expected, actually have *-e-yā-*, as du. 2 *bhare-yā-thām*, etc., i.e., the older form of the stem has been extended by the active major phase of the optative marker. This development has been partially paralleled in the same persons of athematics, where the actual optatives have a stem in *-ī-yā-*, not the expected *-ī-*, as in *bruv-ī-yā́-thām*. But this analogical change is not completely symmetrical; the unextended optative stem did not make its way into the imperfect, but from a misdivision of *-ī-yā-thām*, etc., there emerged neo-secondary med. endings *-ā-thām*, etc. (as *á-bhruv-āthām* etc., for expected **a-bhrū-thām*, etc.). This even generated corresponding primary endings *-āthe*, *-āte*, as med. prs. du. 2 *bruv-ā́the*, etc., for expected **brū-the*.[1] Even more far-reaching recategorizations of optatives as imperfect indicatives occur in Armenian, West Tocharian, and Welsh, see Appendices.

[1] Cf. Kerns-Schwartz. Some duals and optatives in Sanskrit. JAOS 83.205 f.

39. The subjunctive. By late IE proper, the multifunctionality of the injunctive had become inconvenient. Its use in indicative functions was largely obsolete, except in certain petrified forms. A large part of its modal functions were being more and more expressed by the then newly formed optative, but some modal functions continued to be expressed by the injunctive, as the *-s-* aorist injunctive in Skt. pl. 1 *yauṣ-ma* 'separate', or OIr. *-s-* 'subjunctive' sg. 3 *té-is* 'go.' The injunctive forms were partly thematic, as **léi̯qᵘe-t*, aor. **liqᵘé-t*, partly athematic, as in the Sanskrit and Old Irish examples immediately above, as also prs. sg. 3 **es-t* (Ved. pl. 3 *san*) and especially aorists of the *-ē-*, *-ā-* suffixal type. A morphologically unambiguous category next emerged by an exchange of certain stem finals, e.g., **lei̯qᵘē-t* or **lei̯qᵘā-t*, aor. **liqᵘē-t* or **liqᵘā-t* following an athematic model, but **ese-t* etc., following a thematic model. This is the late IE proper subjunctive. Its relative recency is shown (1) by its absence in Germanic, Armenian, Baltic, and Slavic, and (2) by the fact that it allows some use of the primary as well as the secondary endings, so Skt. sg. 3 *ása-t(i)*, while in Greek the primaries sweep the field, even Hom. sg. 3 ἔη-σι (-σι < **-ti*). This partial use of primaries was encouraged by the future-tense implications of certain now specifically subjunctive functions, a morphological practice never found in the somewhat older optative. Where the corresponding indicative is a biphasal athematic, all persons of the subjunctive are formed from its major phase.

a. *Sanskrit.* Surviving injunctives with 'subjunctive' function are common in Vedic. Whitney termed these 'improper subjunctives', a fair descriptive title for the period. Morphologically distinct subjunctives are quite common in Vedic, those corresponding to athematic indicatives often showing a stem final subjunctive *-ā-* not only in the sg. 1, du. 1, pl. 1 (where the thematic indicatives also have them), but also eventually in other persons, after the IE *-ē-*, *-ā-* type, as sg. 2 *áyā-s*, sg. 3 *áyā-t*, after the type of subjunctive normally corresponding to thematic indicatives. Subjunctives from non-present stems occur in early Vedic, cf. aor. sbj. sg. 2 *vidā́s* beside aor. ind. *ávidas*; sbj. sg. 3 *neṣat(i)* beside 'augmentless' + injunctive *nais* (note the quantitative ablaut distinction in the stem internal syllable); pf. sbj. sg. 3 *cākánat, vavártati* beside pf. ind. *cakana, vavárta*; fut. sbj. sg. 2 (isolated) *kariṣyā́s* beside fut. ind. *kariṣyási*. In classical Sanskrit the subjunctive disappears, except where it suppletes the missing forms of the ipv. sg. 1, du. 1, and pl. 1.

b. *Greek.* As in Vedic Sanskrit, Homeric Greek shows some short vowel subjunctives in the aorist and perfect stems, but by Attic-Ionic times the *-ē-* type replaces them so that Hom. aor. sbj. pl. 1 θείομεν : Att. θῶμεν. The *-ē-* stem final, however, has been analogically differentiated to become -η- in the sg. 2, 3, and -ω- in the sg. 1, pl. 1, and pl. 3 to match the apportionment of -ει, -ε and -ο/-ω in the thematic present indicative.

c. *Latin.* The thematic subjunctive type (corresponding to the athematic indicatives) survives in a few forms, functionally limited and recategorized 'future indicative', as sg. 2 **ese-s* > *eri-s*, etc., as well as a derivative category, the 'future perfect', sg. 2 *cecineri-s*. Athematic types, both *-ē-* and *-ā-*, occur. The *-ē-* type occurs in the present subjunctive of the first conjugation, as sg. 2 *amē-s* (otherwise von Planta, Kieckers, and others, who see in this an optative), as also in the *-s-* aorists (drastically recast from the present stem) underlying the 'imperfect subjunctive', sg. 2 *essē-s, veherē-s*, etc., and the conflated perfect and aorist stems underlying the 'pluperfect sunjunctive', sg. 2 *fuissē-s, cecinissē-s*. These stems also occur in the recategorized future indicatives of conjs. III and

IV, as III sg. 2 *canē-s*, IV sg. 2 *veniē-s*, pl. 1 *-ēmus* (the retention of *-ē-* in the pl. 1 and 3 is an archaism in contrast to the Greek recasting to -ω-). The *-ā-* subjunctives remain in the presents of conjs. II, III, IV (sg. 2 *vehā-s*, etc.), but also occur in the sg. 1 of the recategorized 'future indicative' of conjs. III and IV, as sg. 1 *veha-m* (the same form could, of course, be present subjunctive). A few present subjunctives and all perfect subjunctives are IE optatives. A few aorist *-ā-* subjunctives survive in OLat. *adven-a-t, attig-a-t,* later adjusted to classical Lat. *adveniat, attingat,* so as to belong to their present system.

d. *P-Italic.* The situation seems to be essentially the same as in Latin, though we have only a few forms. The Oscan present subjunctive Conj. I seems to show *-ā-ē-*, somewhat more archaic than Latin *-ē-*. Umbrian has here *-a-ia-*, apparently a recasting after Conj. IV. The present subjunctives of Conjs. II-IV have stem final *-ā-* as in Latin. The subjunctive forms of the verb 'to be' are optatives, as in Latin. The *-s-* aorist subjunctives have become future indicatives, as **bhuse-t* > Osc., Umb. *fust* 'erit'; an *-ē-* subjunctive to the same verb > Osc. *fusid* 'esset'; an *-ē-* pf. sbj. pl. 3 *tribarakatti-ns* 'aedificaverint' (the underlying perfect stem in *-tt-* is neological). In contrast to the Latin 'perfect subjunctive' (an optative), this is a true subjunctive.

e. *Old Irish.* The IE *-ā-* subjunctives to chiefly uncharacterized thematic stems (as sg. 3 *·bera* : prs. ind. *·beir* < **bheret*) and to non-sigmatic aorist stems (as sg. 3 *·gaba* : prs. ind. **ghabhet* > *gaib*) are lumped together as present subjunctives. Those of the latter type imply an originally distinct archcategory, as do also the *-s-* subjunctives, really injunctive survivals, although thematicized and therefore true subjunctives in certain persons, as inj. sg. 3 **-(s)tei̯gh-s-t* > *·té*, but pl. 3 **-(s)tei̯gh-so-nt* > *·tíasat*. Both have neological imperfect subjunctives patterned after Old Irish imperfect indicatives, themselves of unclear origin, as sg. 3 *·berad, ·bósad*. Whereas both *-ē-* and *-ā-* subjunctives occur in Italic and possibly Sanskrit, and only *-ē-* in Greek (with considerable later recasting), only the *-ā-* occurs in Old Irish.

f. *Tocharian.* The *-ā-* subjunctives, as WT sg. 3 class V *kārsa-m* : prs. ind. sg. 3 *kārsanaṃ* (class VI) occur, but there were also class V indicatives of other verbs inflected like this subjunctive. Indeed, in some cases, the practice arose of using the present of one class as an indicative, and a present or aorist of almost any other class, with or without historical justification, as a subjunctive, hence many unpredictable pairings occur. The personal endings for both moods are the same in each dialect, East (A) and West (B) Tocharian. The *-ē-* subjunctive does not seem to be represented, but some still recognizably IE thematics occur, as ET med. sg. 2 (class III) *nka-tār* : act. prs. sg. 3 (class VIII) *nkä-ṣ*.

g. *Neological subjunctives.* (1) Armenian. The present 'subjunctive' of class I is *beri-ç-em* and seems an extension either of opt. **bheroi̯-* (> **-ey-* > **-ē-*) or *-ē-* subjunctive stem **bherē-*. Either will > Arm. *beri-*. To this is added **-sk(e)-*, the IE sub-lexeme (though also surviving as such with following **-i̯e-* as Arm *-ç̌e-* in prs. sg. 1 *karç̌i-m* : aor. *kareay*) having become an Armenian mood grammeme (indeed a morphological maid-of-all-work, since it occurs as a grammeme in various other categories). It is then inflected like its concurrent present indicative *bere-m, bere-s,* etc., i.e., sbj. *beriç-em, beri-ç-es,* etc. From this is detached the *-içem, -içes* as subjunctive to *em* 'I am' (though this may be a recasting of earlier **eçem*, cf. isolated OLat. fut. sg. 3 *escit* 'erit', pl. 3 *escunt* 'erunt'). The pattern this set up is analogically paralleled though not quite symmetrically in the other conjugations as well: II pass. ind. *berim, beris*, etc., : sbj. *beriçim, beriçis*, etc.; III act. *lam, las*, etc. : sbj. *layçem, layçes*, etc.; IV act. *helum, helus*, etc. : sbj. *heluçum, heluçus*, etc. The aorist subjunctive shows similar extensions of both root and *-ç-*, as root aor. act. ind. sg. 1 *hani* : sbj. *hani-ç*; pass. *hanay* : sbj. *hanay-ç*; aor. act. *sireçi* : sbj. *sireçi-ç* (2) Albanian. All subjunctive forms are introduced by the particle *të*. The forms are identical with the indicative except for sg. 2, 3. Of the three 'regular' conjugations, note the following paradigms:

	I		II		III	
	Indic.	Sbj.	Indic.	Sbj.	Indic.	sbj.
sg. 2	punoǹ	punòjsh	rrit	rrisish	prish	prishish
sg. 3	,,	punojë	,,	rrisi	,,	prishi

40. Voice. The chief Hittite and IE proper implementation of voice was by selective use of personal endings; prs. act. sg. 3 **-ti* > Hit. *-zi*, Skt. *-ti*, Gk. athem., Dor. -τι, Att. -σι (phonological), Lat. *-t*, Goth. *-þ*, etc., : prs. med. Hit. *-ta(ri)*, Skt. *-ta*, Gk. -ται, Lat. *-tur*, Goth. *-da*, etc. For the sg. 2, 3 and pl. 3 the probable prehistory of these and some other endings has been adumbrated in **9** above, with the implication of original voicelessness, and (much later) the extension of 'secondaries' to 'primaries' in both the newly differentiated voices. Note also the extension of med. secondaries by 'impersonal' *-r*, etc., in some languages, Hittite and Latin as above, Phryg. -τορ Toch. *-tär*, etc. The situation thus far described applies only to the *m* conjugation and not necessarily to the other persons and numbers of this conjugation, where the middle : active endings show various structural disparities and are not necessarily of contemporary origin with the sg. 2, 3, pl. 3 group or even with each other. As for the *h* conjugation, it is by no means certain that PIE verbs so inflected formed (1) a preterite active (except in the paradigmatically isolated sg. 2, 3 *-s-* forms); (2) a present middle (in fact, if such verbs were stative, as often claimed [though highly doubtful], a specific middle would have been inappropriate), or (3) still less a preterite middle. Hittite and IE proper used the *h* conjugation in quite different ways, but each eventually developing a fairly symmetrical system of categories (with some point-to-point correspondences), and came to have many neological forms in which the *m* conjugation became somewhat involved. Thus, e.g., the Hit. med. prs. sg. 1 *-hari* (used even in the *m* conjugation!) is obviously the old *h* conjugation sg. 1 in its pre-Hittite form **-ha*, extended by the old impersonal *-r* + primary *-i*. Probably such a form was partly analogical after PIE med. sg. 3 **-to-r*, wherein the first element was specifically medial. PIE **-ha*, eventually specifically active in IE proper, generally preterite, was taken over in Hittite for a med. sg. 1 present and preterite, then differentiated by extension into prs. **-ha-r*, with **-ha* preterite by relegation (cf. Luwian act. prt. sg. 1 *-ha*) and later further extended to prs. *-ha-ri*, prt. *-ha-t(i)*. Meanwhile *-ha* when active present was altered to *-hi* to match the relatively recent primary *-mi*. It is also clear that in the latest form of the Hittite middle preterite *-ti*, the *-i* had lost its specifically presential connotation. In IE proper, on the other hand, the pf. act. sg. 1 **-a*, sg. 3 **-e* developed by-forms extended with deictic *-i*, as sg. 1 **-ai*, sg. 3 **-ei*. These were not at first specifically middle, cf. Lat. sg. 1 *vīdī*, OCS *vědě*, but came to be so used in Skt. sg. 1, 3 *-e*. If this situation ever did exist in pre-Greek, it was recast to med. primary -ται and sg. 1 -μαι, which itself may be a conflation of primary active **-mi* and older middle **-ai* seen in Sanskrit. Similar forms of the sg. 1 occur in Lithuanian and Old Prussian. In the IE proper perfect, originally a biphasal athematic, the minor phase of the stem is expected in the active plural and the entire middle; so, generally, Skt. sg. 1, 3 *riréca*, but act. pl. and med. *riric-*. In Greek, however, except for vestigial forms like *λελιπ-μεν > Hom. λέλιμμεν, the major phase occurs in the active plural, as pl. 1 λελοίπαμεν (the apparent stem extension -α- is analogical after pl. 3 **n̥ti* > *-αντι > -ᾱσι and often uses the *-e-* grade in the middle, as sg. 3 λέλειπται). Most of the other IE proper languages express aorist and perfect middle forms by periphrases, as does even Greek in the case of optatives and subjunctives.

41. Voice neologisms. The IE proper middle voice category sketched immediately above could almost from the beginning be used for the passive function as well. Indeed, this latter use became the norm in Latin and Gothic. But in some languages specifically passive forms are found.

a. *Sanskrit.* An otherwise uncharacterized stem (often an aorist) is extended by accented **-i̯e-/-i̯o-* to Skt. *-ya-* to form a special passive stem, then inflected with middle endings, as act. sg. 3 *bhárati, dádāti, yunakti* (med. *bhárate, dátte, yuŋkté*) : pass. *bhriyáte* (*-ri* probably reflecting a positional allophone of *-r̥-*), *diyáte, yujyáte*. In the other arch-categories middle forms may function as passives, though there is a special aorist passive sg. 3 of type *abhāri*, cf. **24** above.

b. *Greek.* All middle forms can function as passives except the extended *-ē-* aorists, a Greek archcategory, as sg. 2 ἐ-φάνη-ς probably originally active, but by association with such forms as sg. 2 ἐ-δό-θη-ς (with a Greek paradigmatically isolated ending < IE med. **-thēs*, cf. Skt. *á-di-thās* 'thou wast given'), it became functionally passive, descriptively the Greek 'second aorist passive.' Conversely, and in virtue of the same association, since ἐ-φάνη-ς had beside it ἐ-φάνη-ν etc., ἐ-δό-θη-ς developed ἐ-δό-θη-ν etc., in which -θη- came to be regarded as an aorist passive marker, the Greek 'first aorist passive.' Future passives are developed from both, e.g., sg. 1 φανή-σο-μαι, δο-θή-σο-μαι.

c. *Celtic.* Original middles are now wholly deponent, and the passive function is discharged by impersonals with the logical subject as an object, as NWelsh *cerir fi* 'one loves me' for 'I am loved.'

d. *Armenian.* In the present system verbs with stem final *-i-* (Meillet's second class) are passive, as sg. 1 *ber-im* : act. *ber-em*. This stem final may be related to the Sanskrit passive *-yá-*. As for the aorist stems, *-ē-* suffixal aorists are active, as pl. 3 **e-dhē-nt* (major phase extended in pre-Armenian for earlier **e-dhə-nt*) > Arm act. *e-di-n*, whereas *-ā-* suffixal aorists > Armenian passives, as pl. 3 *han-a-n* 'they were killed' : prs. act. sg. 1 *dne-m, hane-m*. Inflectionally this model is followed in the neological *-ç-* aorists (cf. **31**), as act pl. 3 *sireçi-n* 'they loved' : pass. *sireç̌a-n*. This apportionment of suffixal *-ē-* and *-ā-* aorists recalls the Baltic situation, wherein *-e-* preterites are often transitive, *-a-* preterites mostly intransitive (**23**).

e. *Baltic.* Where there is no preverb, enclitic *-s* (the reflexive pronoun) is added to form a quasi-passive/deponent, as sg. 3 *kẽlė-s* 'he/she raised self, rose' (with preverb the reflexive is infixed after the preverb, *at-si-kėlė*). More than this, the actual personal endings are quantitatively long or diphthongal before the added *-s*, and though some of these may be analogical, others are probably earlier of the voiceless category (see **9** above), as athematic sg. 1 *-mie-s* < **-mai* (cf. Gk. -μαι) + enclitic. Stang [1] regards athem. sg. 1 *-mi* as a regular phonological shortening of *-mie-* in absolute finality, whereas Brugmann and others equate it with IE primary active *-mi*. If Stang is right, his view points to some vestigial functional survival of the voiceless category in Baltic.

f. *Slavic*. OCS also used forms with the reflexive personal pronoun as quasi-passives. But apart from this, sg. 3 *-tъ*, pl. 3 *-$_{<}$*tъ* (more common than *-tь*, -$_{<}$*tь*) may be < IE **-to*, **-nto*, again a partial survival of voicelessness.

g. *Albanian*. In the present stem system a partially coalesced periphrasis with shortened forms of the verb 'to be' is used as a second member; the first member is now, at least, a form of the present stem probably once a verbal noun or adjective. In the preterite, passives are made with the prefix *u-*, as sg. 1 *dërgova* 'I sent' : pass. *u-dërgova*, the *u-* (Meyer § 126) ultimately < **su̯e-* recategorized as a prefixal grammeme.

[1] *Op. cit.*, fn. 17, p. 406.

APPENDICES

Hittite. One stem system, forming presents, preterites, and imperatives in two voices, active and medio-passive (the latter not discussed here). On the basis of the singular personal endings two conjugations must be recognized, one with sg. 1 *-hi*, sg. 2 *-ti*, sg. 3 *-i* ('*h*' conj.), the other normally with *-mi, -si, -ti* ('*m*' conj.). For the *m* conj. the preterite is, in part, the old injunctive, earlier perhaps with singular endings consistently *-m, -s, -t*, but with analogical alterations in some of its verbs, particularly the athematics; in the present and, to some extent the imperative, these old endings are extended by enclitic *i* and *u* respectively, thus generating the 'primary' endings *-mi, -si, -ti*, pl. 3 *-anzi*, and the ipv. sg. 3 *-tu*, pl. 3 *-ntu*. Although the *h* conjugation also developed the same full complement of tenses, it did not do so in the same way. To begin with, we may conjecture that its singular endings had earlier been **-ha, *-ta, *-e* (this conjecture based upon the actual Sanskrit and Greek perfect endings), at first temporally ambivalent, but that after the emergence of *m* conj. specifically present *-mi, -si, *-ti* > *-zi*, when it was desired to create specifically present forms in the *h* conj., the inherited **-ha*, etc. was altered to *-hi, -ti* (for non-assibilation see § **15**), *-i*; note that this is only an alteration, not the suffixation of an enclitic. At least two of the unaltered forms continued in use in various Anatolian languages as specifically preterital by relegation, as sg. 1 *-ha* in HH *asnu-ha*, Luw. *tapar-ha*, sg. 2 *-ta* in Hit. *sak-ta*. But when specific preterites were desired for the *h* conj., there was also an older (?) and morphologically quite different implementation available at least in the sg. 3, namely a tense marker *-s* (of unknown origin) added directly to the stem, and preceding whatever ending (if any!) was to be added; often, apparently, there was none, as in *aks* 'he died' : *aki* 'he dies.' At this point confusion arose; this preterital marker *-s* physically resembled an *m* conj. prt. sg. 2 *-s* common in injunctives (later specifically preterital), and the *h* conj. sg. 2 *-ta* resembled various *m* conj. sg. 3 forms, giving rise to the occasional use of *-s* as a sg. 2 and of *-ta* as a sg. 3, and of a conflated ending *-s-ta* used either as sg. 2 or sg. 3. Confusion was worse confounded by the fact that the *m* conj. contained both athematic and thematic stems, whereas the *h* conj. stems were all athematic. Some *m* conj. athematic stems used prs. sg. 2 forms in *-ti*, prt. sg. 2 *-ta*. Further complicated developments took place in the sg. 1; the *m* conj. sg. 1 **-m* (postconsonantally **-m̥*) infiltrated the *h* conj. not merely in the form **-an*, but also in the form *-un* (this apparently from *nu-* formant stems as **-(n)un*). All of these became confused, *-un* establishing itself in some verbs, *-nun* in others, and a conflation of older **-ha* + *-un* > *-hun* in still others. The forms *-un* and *-nun* infiltrated the *m* conj. athematics and thematics respectively, so that presumable earlier **es-an, *task-an* were replaced by *es-un, taske-nun*. Plural inflections are the same in both conjugations.

The general patterns of both the *h* and *m* inflections were in existence before the cleavage of PIE into Anatolian and IE proper, though the *m* pattern had become the more popular and some shifts in its direction may already have been taking place. In IE proper, for any stems that were henceforth to be present stems, this shift was mandatory, otherwise they would have become perfects (**16**). Thus the PIE preforms of Hit. sg. 1 *tahhi* and characterized stems in *-nahhi* > IE **dō̆-m(i)*, **-nā̆-m(i)*; henceforth IE proper does not admit suffix-characterized perfects, except where the formant of a characterized present has later been extended to the whole paradigm. These considerations may possibly help to explain the difficulty of correlating Hittite stem types of the *h* conjugation with parts of our listing in **13**.

Also before the cleavage into Anatolian and IE proper, but within the *m* inflectional pattern, the distinction between athematics and B-type thematics had at least begun to emerge, (why in the *h* pattern nothing comparable to this dichotomy ever emerged is puzzling, but is too complex for discussion here). At all events, there is no inordinate difficulty in correlating Hittite *m* inflected stem types with IE proper present-stem types. The outstanding correlations are: a. Athematic. Hit. *esmi* (type 1), for minor phase, cf. **4** and fn. 7; *harnenkmi* (type 4), major phase **harnek-* and minor phase **harnk-* and minor phase **harnk-* conflated to monophasal *harnenk-*; *arnumi* (type 6), falling together of both phases, or generalization of one. b. Thematic. *taskemi* (type 12 B); *wemiyami* (type 21).

In the following paradigms, expected but unattested forms are bracketed.

Present

ta- 'take' sg. 1 tahhi, 2, tatti, 3, tai; pl. 1 tummeni, 2. tatteni, 3. tanzi.
tarna- 'put in' tarnahhi, [tarnatti], tarnai; tarnummeni, tarnatteni, tarnanzi.
es- 'be' esmi, [esti], eszi; [esweni], [esteni] asanzi.
harnenk- 'destroy' harnenkmi, harnenkti, harnenkzi; harnenkweni, harnenkteni, harnenkanzi.
arnu- 'bring' arnumi, arnusi, arnuzi; arnummeni, arnutteni, arnuwanzi.
peske- 'give' peskemi [peskesi], peskezi; peskaweni, [peskatteni], peskanzi.
wemiya- 'find' wemiyami, wemiyasi, wemiyazi; [wemiyaweni], [wemiyatteni], wemiyanzi.

Preterite

tahhun, [tas, tatta, tasta], tas[, tatta, tasta]; [tawen], [tatten], tair.
tarnahhun, tarnas[, -tta, -sta], tarnas(ta)[, tarnatta]; tarnuwen, tarnatten, tarnair.
esun, esta, esta; eswen, esten, eser.
harnenkun, harnenkta, harnenkta; [harnenkwen], [harnenkten], harnenkir.
arnunun, [arnut], arnut; [arnummen], [arnutten], arnuir.
peskenun, [peskes], [pesket]; [peskawen], [pesketten], pesker.
wemiyanun, [wemiyat], wemiyat; wemiyawen, wemiyatten, wemiyair.

Imperative

sg. 2 ta, sg. 3 tau; pl. 2 tatten, pl. 3. tantu.
tarna, tarnau; tarnatten, [tarnantu]
es, estu; esten, asantu
harnenk, [harnenktu]; harnenkten, harnenkantu.
arnut, arnutu; [arnutten], arnuantu.
sg. 2 peske, sg. 2 wemiya, etc.

A rare ipv. sg. 1 in -lu-! etc. is a Hit. (perhaps Anatolian) neologism. Unclear.

Sanskrit. Four stem systems: present, aorist, perfect, and future, all inflected in two voices (active and mediopassive, with one isolated specifically passive form, an aor. sg. 3), and mostly in five moods: injunctive, indicative, imperative, optative (with a neological variant, the precative), and subjunctive. In VSkt. the injunctive still occurs even modally; when so used Whitney calls it the 'improper subjunctive.'

Present stems were grouped by the native grammarians (from ca. 350 B.C.) in ten classes of 'primary' verbs, partly according as they were athematic or thematic, the latter with distinction of accentual types A and B (**13**), showing the persistence of the IE accentual system (later replaced by a different one in CSkt.), and partly, though not very consistently, according to the presence or absence of various formants whose earlier specific functions seem to have faded. The grammarians also recognized five 'secondary' characterized present-stem types whose specific functions were perhaps still apparent to them (for these, see below). We list first, in abbreviated form, the ten primary classes with the numbering of the native grammarians, though not in their order (for examples, details, etc., see the table of typical principal parts below): II, simple (i.e. uncharacterized biphasal athematics); III, reduplicated biphasal athematics; VII, biphasal athematics with infixal IE *-né-/-n-́* > Skt. *-ná-/-n-́*; V, biphasal athematics with suffixal IE *-néu̯-/-nu-* > Skt. *-nó-/-nu-*; VIII, same with apparently suffixal Skt. *-ó-/-u-* (mostly disguised instances of V, as IE **tn̥-néu̯-* > Skt. *ta-nó-*, misanalyzed by the native grammarians as *tan-ó-*); IX, biphasal athematics with suffixal IE *-nā̆(i)-/-nə(i)-* > Skt. *-nā́-/-nī-*; I, thematics of accentual type A, some with formants, but none with suffixal IE *-i̯e-* > Skt. *-ya-*; VI, thematics of accentual type B, some with formants, but none with Skt. *-ya-*; IV, thematics with suffixal Skt. *-ya-* and of accentual type A (this because of post-IE retraction of accent); X, thematics with suffixal IE *-ei̯e-* > Skt. *-áya-* (consistency would require these to be listed among the secondaries, since they are partly causatives, partly denominatives with altered accent). The 'secondaries' are: passive, thematics with suffixal *-yá-* (accentual types B); intensive, biphasal athematics with 'heavy' reduplication; desiderative, reduplicated thematics with suffixal IE *-se-* > Skt. *-sa-* or *-iṣa-*; causative, with suffixal *-áya-*; denominatives, thematics with suffixal *-yá-*, formed to noun and adjective stems. Note that secondaries normally coexist with one or more primaries, as primary I sg. 3 *váha-ti* : pass. *uhyá-te*, intens. *vāvahī-ti*, desid. *vivakṣa-ti*, causat. *vāhaya-ti*; with these may be listed the denominatives, as (to noun *deva-s*), *devayá-ti*. Note also that while aorists, perfects, and futures may be formed (or periphrastically suppleted) to secondaries (except passives, for whose non-present stem categories the mediopassives of the corresponding primary are used), they are mostly formed in predictable ways, i.e., the secondaries are 'weak' verbs.

Aorist stems are grouped by Whitney in seven classes (not of course individually concurrent with particular present classes), the first three of which do not contain tense-marker *s* in any form: 1, simple athematics, originally no doubt biphasal, but now partly monophasal, concurrent with various presents; 2, simple thematics, often concurrent with presents having either different stem-internal ablaut or a formant, as prs. I *rocati*, VI *siñcáti* : aor. *arucat, ásicat*; 3, similar to 2 but reduplicated; a few of these, mostly with *a*-redupl, as prs. I *pátati*, III *vívakti* : aor. *ápaptat*. **avaucat* > *ávocat*, like Gk. aor. ἔπεφνον *ἐϝεϝεπον > εἶπον probably date from IE times, but the great bulk, mostly with *-ī̆-*, *-ū̆-*

redupl. variously but systematically distributed, are obviously of much later origin, being Skt. extensions of class 2 aorists, as to aors. *árucat, asicat* just noted, aor. 3 *árūrucat*, and native gram. *asīṣicat*; this later group has definitely causative function, and thus (though morphologically quite different) occurs as aor. to causative presents of type *rocáyati, secayati*; 4, *s-* aorists, mostly late IE or pre-Skt. extensions (using an old PIE *s-* marker attested in certain sg. 2, 3 forms of the Hittite *h* conjugation preterite) of older lengthened grade athematic aorists, as to prs. I *bhárati* older IE **e-bhēr-m̥* (for this, cf. Goth. prt. pl. 1 *bērum*) > pre-Skt. **ábhāram* (ending analogically altered) extended to *ábhārṣam*. In VSkt. there are many sg. 2, 3 forms like *ábhār* which, though conventionally explained < **abhārs-s, *abhārs-t*, may equally well continue older **abhār-s, *abhār-t* (lengthened grade aors. under Whitney's class 1), later such forms are replaced by analogical *abhārṣī-s, abhārṣī-t*; 5, *iṣ-* aorists. In some of these *i* is probably historically not part of a suffixal grammeme, but a lexeme final IE *ə* > Skt. *i*, though with some analogical spreading; 6, *siṣ-* aorists, a rare type, monodialectally a conflation of types 4 and 5; and 7, *(k)ṣa-* aorists, an *s* extension of class 2 aors., as to prs. I *róhati*, aor. 2 *áruhat*, aor. 7 *árukṣat*. This *s-* extension, unlike that in class 4, occurs only when the former pre-stem final consonant is one which can produce cluster *kṣ*. Perhaps an early fortuitous grouping of a few such inhibited further expansion of this type from including others in which cluster *kṣ* would not be produced. There is also the morphologically isolated and apparently endingless sg. 3 aor. pass. of type *abhāri*, etc., see **24**.

Perfect stems are normally reduplicated biphasal athematics, with retention of the old phase distributions, as, to prs. VII *riṇákti*, maj. ph. *rirec-*, minor ph. *riric-*. There are some 'irregularities' in reduplication. Major phases with stem-internal *a* in an open syllable lengthen the vowel in the sg. 3 and sometimes also in the sg. 1; those with stem-final *ā* extend this to *au* in sg. 1, 3 (probably monodialectal, but cf. App. 4, 6); in instances like maj. ph. *yayắm-* : minor ph. **ya-im-* > *yem-* the redupl. of the min. ph. is disguised and this type of min. ph. spreads analogically to some forms where it is not phonologically warranted, as VSkt. analogical min. ph. *pet-* beside phonologically 'correct' *papt-*. To a considerable extent both phases, if ending in a consonant and with a prosodically long final syllable, are extended by an analogical *i*, as pl. 1 *papt-i-má* beside unextended *yuyuj-má*. Finally, several of the endings used in the perfect indicative itself are distinctive, because they come from the old *h* conjugation as sg. 1, 3 *-a*; these occur nowhere else, even in categories formed from the perfect stem, as pf. sg. 1 *jagrábh-a*, but plpf. sg. 1 *ájagrabham*, and cf. pf. opt. sg. 1 *riricyắ-m*.

Future stems are thematic, type 8, with suffixal IE **si̯e* > Skt. *sya* or *-iṣya-*; the *i* of the latter, like that of the aorists of class 5, probably spread analogically from examples with lexeme-final *ə* > *i*. Whether this *s-* future is related to the *s-* aorists is a moot point; we incline to think it is not, particularly because Baltic has an *s-* future, but no *s-* aorists. It may be related to the desideratives, as a large group of Old Irish futures certainly is. The future stem is also used as an 'imperfect future' or 'conditional' neo-category, as, to prs. I *bhárati*, fut. *bhariṣyáti* ipf. fut. *ábhariṣyat*, i.e., 'was about to, would.'

It was the practice of the native grammarians to abstract from the whole mass of forms belonging to a single verb, and under their own notions of ablaut, consonantal developments, etc., a so-called root (in their usage, always monosyllabic), as from prs.

riṇakti, aor. *aricat*, pf. *rireca*, fut. *rekṣyati*, etc., a root *ric*, and in speaking of a particular verb it is this 'root' that they cite, rather than any particular paradigmatic form. If Greek and Latin grammarians had followed this practice, they would not have spoken of the 'verbs' λείπω and *linquō*, but of the 'roots' λιπ- and *liqu-*. Note that in Skt., particularly in VSkt., it is common for several different present and aorist stems (more rarely perfect and future stems) to be formed to the same root, and this situation, partially paralleled in Greek and elsewhere, no doubt continues an IE proper situation. As a practical matter, note that Skt. dictionaries, even those composed by Occidentals, list verbs by their 'roots', and rubricate their preverbal compounds under the simplex; if Greek and Latin dictionaries were so arranged, one would look up e.g., *suscipiō* under a root *cap-*, ἀναβαίνω under βα-.

Typical Principal Parts

The forms given are sg. 3 active (normally ending in prs. and fut. *-ti*, aor. *-t*, pf. *-a* (sometimes *-au*). The minor phases are listed without ending; in the actual attachment of endings, phonological adjustments are sometimes necessary. The Skt. root is given with Whitney (Roots) page reference; the Roman numeral is the native grammarian present-stem class; the Arabic numerals in parentheses refer to the types in **13**; under aorists the numbers are the Whitney classification; = indicates monophasality; + indicates the occurrence of other forms (types, classes) to the same root.

Present	Aorist	Perfect	Future
as 5 II ás-ti/s-́ (1)	——	ā́s-a / =	
i 7 é-ti / i-́ (1)	1. opt. ī-yā-t	iyā́y-a/īy-	eṣya-ti
rud 142 II ródi-ti/rud- (2)	2. á-ruda-t +	rurod-a/rurud-	rodiṣya-ti
brū 107 II bravī-ti/brū- (2)	1. prec. brū-yās-ta	———	———
hu 206 III juhó-ti/juhu- (3) +	4. á-hauṣī-t +	juhāv-a/juhu- +	hoṣyá-ti
yuj 132 VII yunák-ti/yuñj- (4) +	4. a-yokṣī-t +	yuyój-a/yuyuj-	yokṣya-ti
su 187 V sunó-ti/sun(u)- (6) +	3. pl. 3 a-suṣav-ur	suṣā́v-a/suṣu-	soṣya-ti
ġrabh 40 IX gr̥bhṇā́-ti/gr̥bhṇ(ī)- (5) +	3. a-jigrabha-t +	jagrā́bh-a/jagr̥bh-	grahīṣya-ti
vr̥t 164 I varta-ti (8A)	1. á-var-t +	vǎvárt-a/vǎvr̥t-	vartsyá-ti
diś 73 VI diśá-ti (8B)	7. a-dikṣa-t +	didéś-a/didiś-	dekṣya-ti
muc 122 VI muñcá-ti (10B)	1, 4? á-mauk +	mumóc-a/mumuc-	mokṣya-ti

Selected Paradigms (indicative active only)

The reader will note many 'irregularities', some of them mere phonological adjustments which he will understand as such, and others more serious, for which he may turn to the special grammars.

Present

II sg. 1 ás-mi, ás-i, ás-ti; du. 1 s-vás. s-thás, s-tás; pl. 1 s-más, s-thá, s-ánti
é-mi, -ṣi, -ti; i-vás, -thás, -tás; -más, -thá, y-ánti

III	juhó-mi, -ṣi, -ti; juhu-vás, -thás, -tás; -más, -thá, júhv-ati
	dádā·mi, -si, -ti; dad-vás, dat-thás, -tás; dad-más, dat-thá, dád-ati
VII	yunáj-mi, yunak-ṣi, -ti; yuñj-vás, yuŋk-thás, -tás; yuñj-más, yuŋk-thá, yuñj-anti
I	sī́dā-mi, sī́da-si, -ti; sī́dā-vas, sī́da-thas, -tas; sī́dā-mas, sī́da-tha, -nti
VI	diśā́-mi, diśā́-si, -ti; diśā́-vas, diśá-thas, -tas; diśā́-mas, diśá-tha, -nti

I and VI differ only in VSkt. accent

Imperfect

II	ā́s-am (sg. 2, 3 VSkt. ā́s; CSkt. ā́sī-s, -t); ā́s-va, -tam, -tām; -ma, -ta, -an
	ā́y-an, ái-s, -t; -va, -tam, -tām; -ma, -ta, ā́y-an
III	á-juhav-am, á-juho-s, -t; á-juhu-va, -tam, -tām; -ma, -ta, á-juhav-ur,
	á-dadā-m, -s, -t; á-dad-va, á-dat-tam, -tām; á-dad-ma, á-dat-ta, á-dad-ur
VII	á-yunaj-am, sg. 2, 3 á-yunak; á-yuñj-va, á-yuŋk-tam, -tām; -yuñj-ma, -yuŋk-ta, -yuñj-an
I	á-sīda-m, -s, -t; á-sīdā-va, á-sīda-tam, -tām; á-sīdā-ma, á-sīda-ta, á-sīda-n
VI	á-diśa-m, etc. (VSkt. accent as in I ásīdam)

Aorist

1. athem	á-dā-m, -s, -t; -va, -tam, -tām; -ma, -ta, á-d-ur
2. them	á-sada-m, etc. as ipf. I ásīdam
3. them	á-sīṣada-m, etc. as ipf. I ásīdam
4. athem	á-bhārṣ-am (sg. 2, 3 VSkt. á-bhār, CSkt. á-bhārṣī-s, -t); -va, -tam, -tām; -ma, -ta, -ur
5. athem	á-bodhiṣ-am, á-bodhī-s, -t; á-bodhiṣ-va, etc. as class 4
6. athem	á-yāsiṣ-am, á-yāsī-s, -t, etc. as class 4
7. them	á-dikṣa-m, etc. as ipf. I á-sīda-m

Perfect

rud 142 rurod-a, -i-tha, rurod-a; rurud-i-va, rurud-athur, -atur; rurud-i-ma, rurud-a, -ur
sad 183 sasád-a, sasát-tha, sasā́d-a; sed-i-va, sed-athur, -atur; sedi-má, sed-á, -ur
dā 71 dadáu, dadā́-tha, dadáu; dadi-vá; dad-áthur, -átur; dadi-má, dad-á, -úr

Pluperfect

Rare, and VSkt only, examples: sg. 1 ájagrabh-am; sg. 2 *á-jagam-s and sg. 3 *á-jagam-t, both > á-jagan; du. 2 á-mumuk-tam; pl. 2 á-jagan-ta; pl. 3 á-cucyav-ur

Future

dāsyā́-mi, bhariṣyā́-mi, etc. as them. prs. VI diśā́-mi

Future Imperfect, or Conditional

á-dāsya-m, á-bhariṣya-m, etc. as them. ipf. ádiśam

Mood Formation

Non-indicative moods occur only for the present, aorist, and perfect tenses, with one isolated instance of a future subjunctive. Insofar as stem formation for moods is concerned, much of what is stated here applies equally to the mediopassive, but all examples cited are active.

Injunctive. This is the category underlying indicative imperfects and aorists; in the case of the perfect there is no inherited injunctive, but one can be hypothesized from the pluperfect indicative. When augment is added to the injunctive, the augment carries the accent and the form has thereby become an indicative; without augment the original accent obtains, so VII ipf. ind. sg. 3 *á-riṇak*, aor. (4) *á-bhār*, aor. (2) *á-sadat* : inj. *riṇák*, *bhā́r*, *sádat*. What most grammars call 'augmentless' imperfects, aorists, or pluperfects are really injunctives used factually, not modally.

Imperative. In so far as it is morphologically a distinct category, the imperative is based on the injunctive. In athematics the sg. 2 uses the minor phase, otherwise the phase distribution is as in the injunctive and indicative. The sg. 2 of most athematics has a personal ending *-dhi* (or its dialect variant *-hi*), as II *i-hí*, *juhu-dhí*, VII *yuŋg-dhí*, aor. (1) *kr̥-dhí*, pf. *mumug-dhí* : corresponding inds. *é-ṣi*, *juhō-ṣi*, *yunák-ti*, *akar* (loss of *-s*), **mumoci-tha*; II **az-dhi*, III **daz-dhi* > *e-dhí*, *de-hí* somewhat anomalous. Sometimes in class V, but regularly in all thematics, the sg. 2 is endingless, as V *kr̥ṇu-hí* and *kr̥ṇú*, but only *sunú*, I *sī́da*, aor. (2) *ruhá*, *sáda* : corresponding inds. prs. *kr̥ṇó-ṣi*, *sunó-ṣi*, *sī́da-si*, aor. (2) *áruha-s*, *ásada-s*. The sg. 3 and pl. 3 add a mood-marking enclitic *-u* to the injunctive forms (whose earlier endings *-t*, *-(e)nt* had not yet been lost or reduced), thus:

ipv. sg. 3	ás-tu pl. 3 s-ántu; é-tu, y-ántu; III juhó-tu, júhv-atu; dádā-tu, dád-atu
ind.	ás-ti s-ánti; é-ti, y-ánti; juhó-ti, júhv-ati; dádā-ti, dád-ati
ipv. VII	yunák-tu, yuñj-ántu; V sunó-tu, sunv-ántu; aor. (1) dā́-tu
ind.	yunák-ti, yuñj-ánti; sunó-ti, sunv-ánti; á-dā-t
pf. ipv.	mumók-tu them. prs. sī́da-tu, sī́da-ntu; aor. (2) sáda-tu
pf. ind.	mumóc-a ind. sī́da-ti, sī́da-nti; ásada-t

In the du. 2, 3 and pl. 2 the injunctive forms are used without change as imperatives, except that in VSkt. the pl. 2 ipv. ending is sometimes extended by *-na*, as *-tana*, an extension also found in the indicative present and imperfect, but far less frequently. The rare *-tāt* (< IE sg. abl. *tōd*?) attached directly to the stem was occasionally used in VSkt. not only for the sg. 2, but on occasion in other persons and numbers (even the sg. 1!).

Optative. Athematic indicative stems build this mood by extending the minor phase with *-yā*, itself earlier probably biphasal with minor phase *-ī*, still to be observed in the mediopassive; the optative stem thus formed is now monophasal. To thematics the mood is built by extending stem-final *-a* + opt. marker *-i*, yielding *-e*. Secondary endings are used for both, and the series are:

(to athem. inds.) -yā-m, -yā-s, -yā-t; -yā-va, -yā-tam, -yā-tām; -yāma, -yā-ta, -y-ur
(to them. inds.) -ey-am, -e-s, -e-t; -e-va, -e-tam, -e-tām; -e-ma, -e-ta, -ey-ur

Thus, sg. 3 prs. II *s-yā-t*; aor. (1) *bhū-yā-t*; pf. *vavr̥t-yā-t*; prs. I *sī́d-e-t*, VI *diś-é-t*; aor. (2) pl. 1 *vid-é-ma*, *sád-e-ma*. The '*precative*', a specifically Sanskrit neological variant of the optative (not functionally distinct from it), is built by extending athematic aorist stems in *-yā-* by *-s-*, as sg. 1 *-yā-s-am*, etc. Only a few occurrences are cited.

Subjunctive. (Cf. **39** a) Where the stem of corresponding indicatives is athematic, its major phase is extended by *-a* (but sg. 1, du. 1, pl. 1 by *-ā*), giving it a thematic appearance, as *as-a-* to ind. *as-*. When the corresponding indicative is thematic, the stem-final *-a* is lengthened to *-ā*, giving it a monophasal athematic appearance, as *sīdā-* to *sīda-*. The endings are somewhat intricate and historically puzzling: the du. 1, pl. 1, pl. 3 always use secondary endings (*-va, -ma, -n*); in the du. 2, 3 and pl. 2 primary endings are used (*-thas, -tas, -tha*); in the sg. 2, 3 both primaries and secondaries are free variants [*-s(i), -t(i)*]; in the sg. 1 use is made of either endingless *-ā* or an extension to *-āni*, probably on the purely phonological analogy of nom.-acc. neut. *a-* stems in Vedic *-ā/-āni* (so substantially, Hirt IG IV, p. 145).

To athem. ind. sg. 3 II as-a-t(i); aor. (5) bódhiṣ-a-t(i); pf. múmoc-a-t(i)
To them. ind. I sī́dā-t(i); aor. (2) sádā-t(i); fut. sg. 2 kariṣyā́-s (almost isolated)

Greek. Six stem systems: Present, active and mediopassive; Aorist, active and middle; Aorist passive; Perfect active; Perfect mediopassive; Future, active and middle. Monodialectal stem alterations and neologisms compel us to recognize distinct aorist-passive and perfect mediopassive systems.

Present. Stems are athematic or thematic, recognizable by their act. sg. 1 endings athem. -μι (mid. -μαι) and them. -ω, phonologically sometimes -ῶ (mid. -ομαι, phonologically sometimes -ῶμαι, -οῦμαι) respectively. Conventionally this is made the chief over-all distinction in classifying verbs (*mi-* verbs and *o-* verbs), though these terms refer only to the present stem. Some aorist stems are athematic, others thematic; all perfect stems, athematic; all future stems thematic; and all this irrespective of their concurrent presents. The table of Typical Principal Parts below illustrates the survival of various IE present-stem types (cf. **13**) and the emergence of some new ones, together with the other stems of various types that have come to be concurrent with these. From such data a rather more detailed classification of verbs is set up than that of the general classification mentioned above, but like that classification (as presented in traditional grammars), reference is made only to present-stem formation. In general the inflections of athematics differ somewhat for many individual verbs, whereas that of all thematics is the same, except that in the case of stem types (19) and (20), i.e., in *-a-i̯e, -e-i̯e,* and the Greek innovating type in *-o-i̯e*, the phonological loss of intervocalic *-i̯-* causes contractions which produce distinct sub-varieties of the general thematic pattern (the 'alpha, epsilon, omicron contracts' of conventional descriptive grammar). The present system includes the present indicative, imperfect indicative, present imperative, present optative, and present subjunctive, all inflected in both the active and mediopassive voices.

Aorist. The aorist active and middle stems are in part IE relegated athematic aorists, cf. **21** (some of these are no longer used in the sg. 1, 2, 3, where they are suppleted by *k-* aorists extended from their obsolete forms, as see below), and in part IE relegated thematic aorists, rarely reduplicated, see **26**, all (except the *k-* aorists) descriptively termed 'second aorists', and those of the first mentioned group further qualified as '*mi-* form second aorists'; and in part IE *s-* aorists. Of these some are perhaps extended from earlier IE lengthened grade aorists, see **22**, others partly analogical in various ways. All of these have a purely phonological sub-group, the 'liquid aorists', in which the morpheme-boundary clusters **-l-s-*, **-r-s-*, **-m-s-*, **-n-s-* are reduced to *-l-*, *-r-*, *-m-*, *-n-* respectively, with consequent lengthening of the stem-internal vocalism. Finally, the *k-* aorists mentioned above are in point of inflection best grouped with the *s-* aorists and liquid aorists. From their sheer numerical preponderance the *s*-aorists, etc., are descriptively termed 'first aorists.' All these various groups and sub-groups are noted in our table as 2 *mi*, 2, 2 *red.*; 1, 1 liq., 1 *k*. The aorist system includes the aorist indicative, aorist imperative, aorist optative, and aorist subjunctive, all active and middle only.

Aorist passive. The stems are in part IE athematic aorists with stem final (if from dissyllabic bases) or quasi-suffixal (if analogical) *ē*, cf. **23**, and in part neologisms based on IE secondary sg. 2 mid. ending *-thēs*. Note that some clusters arising at the morpheme boundary between the old stem-final consonant and initial *th-* of the extension phonologically produce *s-*, as sg. 3 *ἐπείθ-θην > ἐπείσθην and that this *s-* is sometimes analogically extended to other forms without historical justification, as sg. 1 ἐγνώσθην for expected *ἐγνώθην. Note also that such forms as ἐγενήθην with apparent η- extension before θ(: prs. γίγνομαι) may imply earlier aorist *ἐγένην. Those of the first-mentioned group are descriptively termed 'second-aorist' passives, those of the latter 'first-aorist' passives merely from their greater frequency; all these and their sub-groups are noted in our table by 2, 1, 1σ, 1η respectively. The aorist passive system includes the aorist passive indicative, aorist passive imperative, aorist passive optative, aorist passive subjunctive, all inflected with active endings, and the following derivative neo-categories: future passive indicative, as sg. 1 φανήσομαι, δοθήσομαι (to aorist passives ἐφάνην, ἐδόθην) and the corresponding future passive optative, both inflected with middle endings.

Perfect active. Stems are in part of IE type, though showing some alterations in reduplication and stem-internal vocalism. Old phase distinctions are retained only in (unredupl.) sg. 1 οἶδα : pl. 1 ἴσμεν and in a few vestigial Homeric forms, as plpf. pl. 1 *ελέλιπμεν > ἐλέλιμμεν. Attic either generalizes the major phase, as pl. 1 λελοίπαμεν after sg. 1 λέλοιπα or substitutes present-stem vocalism, as πέφευγα for expected *πέφουγα : prs. φεύγω, etc. In this group there are special sub-groups: those with stem-final vowel nowhere showing analogical stem extension, as pl. 1 ἕστα-μεν descriptively qualified as 'of the μι-form', whereas nearly all other perfects of this group have stem extension -α- in the du. 2, 3 and pl. 1, 2, as λελοίπα-μεν; and a sub-group in which we find -φ and -χ for expected -π or -β, -κ or -γ respectively, by analogical spread from a single form, the pl. 2 mid. (!), where e.g., *-π-σθε phonologically > -φ-θε, descriptively termed 'aspirated perfects'; but all groups so far discussed are included in the cover term 'second perfects.' As against them there is a far larger neological group with suffixal -κ- (sg. 3 -κε **18**), termed merely from their greater frequency 'first perfects.' These various groups are noted in our table as 2μ, 2, 2 asp., and 1. The perfect active system includes the perfect active indicative, the pluperfect active indicative (partly inherited, partly neological), rarely also the perfect active imperative, perfect active optative, and perfect active subjunctive, plus isolated instances of two derivative neo-categories: future perfect active indicative, and future perfect active optative, as τεθνήξω, τεθνήξοιμι : pf. τέθνηκα.

Perfect middle. Stems are largely of IE type but must be treated as an arch-category because the concurrent perfect active is so often a 'first active' (the -κ- suffix never occurs in the perfect middle). The stem-internal vocalism is sometimes the expected minor phase, as sg. 3 **tetn̥-tai* > τέτα-ται (: prs. *τενι̯ω > τείνω), sometimes follows the present-stem vocalism, as sg. 3 λέλειπται for expected *λελιπται. Assimilation often occurs between stem-final and ending-initial consonants, as in *ἐλελιπμεν > Hom. ἐλέλιμμεν above; in this connection, as in the aorist passive stem, a neo-stem final -σ sometimes arises phonologically, and sg. 3 *πεπειθ-ται > πέπεισται, analogically extended to sg. 1 πέπεισμαι, and again to some forms without historical justification, as sg. 3 ἔγνωσται for expected *ἔγνωται. An apparent extension -η as in γεγένημαι may have been taken over from aor. pass. ἐγενήθην or its conjectured antecedent *ἐγενην. These points are noted in our table by σ and η respectively. The perfect middle system includes the perfect middle indicative, pluperfect middle indicative, perfect middle imperative (but a functional perfect middle optative and subjunctive, if needed, are suppleted periphrastically), with occasional instances of the derivative neo-categories future perfect middle indicative, and future perfect middle optative, as sg. 1 μεμνήσομαι, μεμνησοίμην to pf. mid. μέμνημαι.

Future active and middle. Stems are mostly IE *-se-* extensions of any convenient stem, as λείψω to prs. λείπω (actually to older athematic *λειπ-μι); if this formation is related to the *s*- aorist, many of these could be old *s*- aorist short-vowel subjunctives (**39**) recategorized as future indicatives. For stem form before the marker -σ-, note apparent borrowings from the aorist passive and the perfect middle and passive, as δήξω (to prs. δάκνω) : aor. pass. ἐδήχθην (earlier *ἐδηκ -?), pf. mid. δέδηγμαι or γενήσομαι (to prs. γίγνομαι) : aor. pass. ἐγενήθην pf. mid. γεγένημαι, etc. The retention of the tense marker -σ- when apparently intervocalic is, of course, phonological in such cases as *τελεσ-σω > τελέσω, but analogical in others, as δώσω (to prs. δίδωμι); in other cases, as *ὀλεσω (to prs. ὄλλυμι) > *ὀλεω > ὀλῶ (sg. 2 ὀλεῖς) and *ἐλασω (to prs. ἐλαύνω) > *ἐλαω > ἐλῶ (sg. 2 ἐλᾷς) it is phonologically lost, and the resulting forms are inflected like 'epsilon and alpha contract' presents, respectively. In Attic this 'epsilon contract' type spreads analogically in futures concurrent with denominative presents in *-ιδιω > -ίζω, as prs. νομίζω, fut. νομιῶ, sg. 2 νομιεῖς, etc., (the so-called Attic futures). Attic has a rare future with marker **-sei̯e-* (conflated from **-se-* and **-si̯e-* (in Sanskrit and Lithuanian, q.v.), as *πετσεο-μαι > πεσοῦμαι (inflected like an 'epsilon contract', as sg. 2 πεσεῖ, etc.) to prs. πέτομαι; this type, however, is common in Doric, and is hence called the 'Doric future.' Finally, fut. sg. 1 ἔδομαι and πίομαι are recategorized short-vowel sunjunctives to probable earlier athematic present indicatives **pī-mi, *ed-mi.* The various minor varieties are noted in our table -εο-, -αο-, -σεο-, subjunctive respectively. The future system includes the future indicative active and middle, and the future optative active and middle.

Typical Principal Parts

Most forms are Attic, sg. 1 active or middle, except as starred or otherwise noted; but occasional non-Attic forms are not typographically distinguished.

Prs.	Aor. act., mid.	Aor. pass.	Pf. act.	Pf. mid., pass.	Fut. act., mid.
φημί (1)	1 ἔφησα				φήσω
εἰμί (1)					ἔσομαι
ἄγαμαι (2)	1 ἠγασάμην	1σ ἠγάσθην			

Prs.	Aor. act., mid.	Aor. pass.	Pf. act.	Pf. mid., pass.	Fut. act., mid.
ἵστημι (3)	2μι ἔστην	1 ἐστάθην	2μι pl. 1 ἕσταμεν	ἕσταμαι	στήσω
	1 ἔστησα		κ ἕστηκα		
δίδωμι (3)	2μι ἔδομεν	1 ἐδόθην	1 δέδωκα	δέδομαι	δώσω
	κ ἔδωκα				
τίθημι (3)	2μι ἔθεμεν pl. 1	1 ἐτέθην	τέθηκα	τέθημαι	θήσω
	κ ἔθηκα				
ἵημι (3)	2μι εἷμεν pl. 1	1 εἵθην	1 εἷκα	εἷμαι	ἥσω
πίμπλημι (3, 4)	1 ἔπλησα	1 ἐπλήσθην	1 πέπληκα	σ πέπλησμαι	πλήσω
	2μι ἐπλήμην				
δάμνημι (5)		2 ἐδάμην		δέδμημαι	
		1 ἐδμήθην			
μάρναμαι (5)					
δείκνῦμι (6)	1 ἔδειξα	1 ἐδείχθην	2 asp. δέδειχα	δέδειγμαι	δείξω
ἕννῦμι (7, 6)	1 ἕσσα +			ἕσμαι +	εο ἑσ(σ)ω +
*ὄλνυμι (6)	1 ὤλεσα		2 ὀλώλεκα		εο ὀλῶ
> ὄλλυμι			1 ὄλωλα		
λείπω (8A)	2 ἔλιπον	1 ἐλείφθην	2 λέλοιπα	*λελειπμαι	λείψω
				> λέλειμμαι	
φεύγω (8A)	2 ἔφυγον		2 πέφευγα		φεύξομαι
πέμπω (8A)	1 ἔπεμψα	1 ἐπέμφθην	2 πέπομφα	*πεπεμπμαι	πέμψω
				> πέπεμμαι	
τέρπω (8A)	1 ἔτερψα	1 ἐτέρφθην			τέρψω
δέρω (8A)	1 liq. ἔδειρα	2 ἐδάρην		δέδαρμαι	εο δερῶ
					sg. 2 -εῖς
φέρω (8A)	1 ἤνεγκα	1 ἠνέχθην	2 asp. ἐνήνοχα	ἐνηνέγμαι	οἴσω
	2 ἤνεγκον				
ἔχω (8A)	2 ἔσχον		ἔσχηκα	ἔσχημαι	ἕξω
τρέπω (8A)	1 ἔτρεψα	2 ἐτράπην	2 τέτροφα +	τέτραμμαι	τρέψω
		1 ἐτρέφθην			
τρέφω (8A)	1 ἔθρεψα	2 ἐτράφην	2 τέτροφα	τέθραμμαι	θρέψω
ἄγω (8A)	2 ἤγαγον	1 ἤχθην	2 ἦχα	ἦγμαι	ἄξω
τίκτω (9)	2 ἔτεκον		2 τέτοχα		τέξομαι
πίπτω (9)	2 ἔπεσον		πέπτωκα		σεο πεσοῦμαι
γίγνομαι (9)	2 ἐγενόμην	1 ἐγενήθην	2 γέγονα	η γεγένημαι	γενήσομαι
λαμβάνω (10,11)	2 ἔλαβον	1 ἐλήφθην	2 asp. εἴληφα	εἴλημμαι	λήψομαι
δάκνω (11)	2 ἔδακον	1 ἐδήχθην	2 asp. δέδηχα	δέδηγμαι	δήξομαι
κάμνω (11)	2 ἔκαμον		1 κέκμηκα		εο καμοῦμαι
τέμνω (11)	2 ἔτεμον	1 ἐτμήθην	1 τέτμηκα	τέτμημαι	εο τεμῶ
τίνω (11)	1 ἔτεισα	1σ ἐτείσθην	1 τέτεικα	σ τέτεισμαι	τείσω
ἐλαύνω (11, 17)	1 ἤλασα	1 ἠλάθην	1 ἐλήλακα	ἐλήλαμαι	αο ἐλῶ
θρώσκω (12)	2 ἔθορον				εο θοροῦμαι
εὑρίσκω (12)	2 ηὗρον +	1 εὑρέθην	1 ηὕρηκα	εὕρημαι	εὑρήσω

Prs.	Aor. act., mid.	Aor. pass.	Pf. act.	Pf. mid., pass.	Fut. act., mid.
ἁλισκομαι (12)	2μι ἑάλων		1 ἑάλωκα		ἁλώσομαι
γίγνώσκω (9, 12)	2μι ἔγνων	1σ ἐγνώσθην	1 ἔγνωκα	σ ἔγνωσμαι	γνώσομαι
διδάσκω (9, 12)	1 ἐδίδαξα	1 ἐδιδάχθην	11 asp. δεδίδαχα	δεδίδαγμαι	διδάξω
δῡ́ω (18)	2μι ἔδῡν	1 ἐδύθην	1 δέδυκα	δέδυμαι	δῡσω
	1 ἔδυσα				
*βαμι̯ω (18)	2μι ἔβην	1 ἐβάθην	1 βέβηκα	βέβαμαι	βήσομαι
> βαίνω					
*φανι̯ω (18)	1 liq. ἔφηνα	2 ἐφάνην	2 πέφηνα	σ πέφασμαι	εο φανῶ
> φαίνω		1 ἐφάνθην			
*βαλι̯ω (18)	2 ἔβαλον	1 ἐβλήθην	1 βέβληκα	βέβλημαι	βαλῶ
> βάλλω					βαλλήσω
*στελι̯ω (18)	1 liq. ἔστειλα	2 ἐστάλην	1 ἔσταλκα	ἔσταλμαι	εο στελῶ
> στέλλω					
*τιμαι̯ω (19)	1 ἐτῑ́μησα	1 ἐτιμήθην	1 τετῑ́μακα	τετῑ́μημαι	τιμήσω
> τιμάω					
*φιλει̯ω (20)	1 ἐφίλησα	1 ἐφιλήθην	1 πεφίληκα	πεφίλημαι	φιλήσω
> φιλέω					
*δηλοι̯ω --	1 ἐδήλωσα	1 ἐδηλώθην	1 δεδήλωκα	δεδήλωμαι	δηλώσω
> δηλόω					
*μεθυι̯ω (22)	1 ἐμέθυσα				
> μεθύω					
*παιδευι̯ω (22)	1 ἐπαίδευσα	1 ἐπαιδεύθην	1 πεπαίδευκα	πεπαίδευμαι	παιδεύσω
> παιδεύω					
ποτέομαι (25)		1 ἐποτήθην		πεπότημαι	

Select Paradigms

This selection seeks to stress contrasts, etc., in stem formation and gives only the roughest general picture of Greek verb morphology; thus, e.g., accentual shifts required by the Greek 'three-syllable law' are frequently disregarded in the abbreviated notation here used. For these and all but the most important points of inflection as distinct from stem formation special grammars must be consulted.

Present

Athem. sg. 1 φη-μί, φή-ς/φῄ-ς, -σί; du. 2, 3 φα-τόν; pl. 1 φα-μέν, -τέ, φασί < *φαντι

('go') εἶ-μι, εἶ, εἶ-σι; ἴ-τον; ἴ-μεν, ἴ-τε, ἴᾱσι

εἰ-μί, εἶ, ἔστι/ἐστί; ἐσ-τόν; ἐσ-μέν, ἐσ-τέ, εἰσί < *ἑντι

Note generalization of maj. ph. except in pl. 3, where smooth breathing is analogical.

ἵστη-μι, -σ, -σι; ἵστα-τον; -μεν, -τε, ἱστᾶσι < *ἱστα-αντι

Note recasting and phonological changes in pl. 3 ending.

δίδω-μι, -ς, -σι; δίδο-τον; -μεν, -τε, διδό-ασι, similarly τίθη-μι

Note analogical recasting of min. ph. διδο- < *διδα- < IE *didə-; similarly τιθε- < *dhidhə-.

δείκνυ-μι, -ς, -σι; δείκνῠ-τον; -μεν, -τε, -ᾱσι

Note analogical recasting of maj. ph. formant -νῡ- < IE *-neu̯-.

Themat. λείπω, λείπεις, λείπει; λειπέ-τον; λείπο-μεν, λείπε-τε, λείπουσι < *λειποντι

Note the stem-final variation ε/ο etc.; sg. 2, 3 much discussed but unclear.

τιμά-ω/τιμ-ῶ, -ᾷς, -ᾷ; -ᾶ-τον; -ῶ-μεν, -ᾶ-τε, -ῶσι

i.e., *-āi̯ō > -άω > -ῶ, -άεις > -ᾷς etc., in 'alpha contracts.'

φιλέ-ω/φιλ-ῶ, -εῖς, -εῖ; -εῖτον; -οῦμεν, -εῖτε, -οῦσι

i.e., *-ei̯ō > -έω > -ῶ, -έεις > -εῖς etc., in 'epsilon contracts.'

δηλό-ω/δηλ-ῶ, -οῖς, -οῖ; -οῦ-τον; -οῦ-μεν, -τε, -σι

i.e., neological *-oi̯ō > -όω > -ῶ, -όεις > -οῖς etc., in 'omicron contracts.'

Imperfect (note distinction of du. 2 and du. 3)

Athem. ἔφη-ν, -σθα, *-τ > ἔφη; du. 2 ἔφᾰ-τον, du. 3 ἐφά̆-την; ἔφα-μεν, -τε, -σαν

sg. 2 -σθα (with misanalysis) from ἦσ-θα and pf. οἶσ-θα below; pl. 3 -σαν from first aorist, cf. below.

ἦ/ἦν, ἦσ-θα, ἦν; ἦσ-τον, ἤσ-την; ἦ-μεν, ἦ(σ)-τε, ἦ-σαν

maj. ph. generalized as in the present; sg. 1 ἦ fallen together < IE (augmented) ipf. *ēsm̥- and (redupl.) pf. *ēs-a (cf. Skt. ipf. ā́s-am, pf. ā́s-a); sg. 1 ἦν later recasting; sg. 3 ἦν (Hom. ἦεν) recategorized from pl. 3 IE *ēs-ent; pl. 3 ἦσαν a later analogy, cf. ἔφασαν above.

ἵστη-ν, -ς, *-τ > ἵστη; ἵστα-τον, -την; -μεν, -τε, -σαν

Note disguised augment and displaced rough breathing.

ἐδείκνῡ-ν, -ς, *-τ > ἐδείκνῡ; ἐδείκνυ-τον, -την; -μεν, -τε, -σαν

Themat. ἔλειπον, ἔλειπε-ς, *-τ > ἔλειπε; -τον, -την; ἐλείπ-ο-μεν, -ε-τε, -ο-ν

ἐτί̄μω-ν, -ᾱ-ς, -ᾱ; -ᾶ-τον, -ά̄-την; -ῶ-μεν, -ᾶ-τε, -ω-ν

ἐφίλ-ου-ν, -ει-ς, -ει; -εῖ-τον, -εί-την; -οῦ-μεν, -εῖ-τε, -ου-ν

ἐδήλ-ου-ν, -ου-ς, -ου; οῦ-τον, -ού-την; -οῦ-μεν, -οῦ-τε, -ου-ν

Aorist Active

prs. ἵστημι ἔστη-ν, -ς, *-τ > ἔστη; -τον, -την; -μεν, -τε, -σαν

Note generalization of major phase; pl. 3 -σ-αν < first aorists.

prs. δίδωμι sg. recast, see ἔδωκα below; ἔδο-τον, -την; -μεν, -τε, -σαν with min. ph. -ο- for expected -α- < IE -ə-

prs. λείπω ἔλιπο-ν, etc., as ipf. ἔλειπον above

prs. τιμάω ἐτί̄μησ-α, -ας, -ε; -ατον, -άτην; -αμεν, -ατε, -αν

sg. 1 -α < *-m̥; pl. 3 -α-ν < *-n̥t extended by -ν from other tenses; these two evoked a stem-extension -α- in all other persons and numbers except sg. 3 -ε, which probably follows the perfect.

prs. φαίνω ἔφηνα etc., as ἐτί̄μησα above

prs. δίδωμι — ἔδω-κ-α, -ας, -ε; du. and pl. above
Recast from expected *ἐ-δω-ν; -κα etc., after first perfects; aor. -κ- forms, largely restricted to active singular.

Aorist Passive

prs. φαίνω — ἐφάνη-ν, -ς, *-τ > ἐφάνη; -τον, -την; -μεν, -τε, -σαν

prs. δίδωμι — ἐδόθη-ν etc., as ἐφάνην above

Future Passive (with medio-passive endings!)

prs. φαίνω — φανήσο-μαι, φανήσῃ/φανήσει, φανήσε-ται; -σθον; φανησό-μεθα, φανήσε-σθε φανήσο-νται

prs. δίδωμι — δοθήσο-μαι etc., as φανήσομαι above

Perfect Active

non-redupl. — οἶδ-α, οἶσ-θα, οἶδ-ε; ἴσ-τον; -μεν, -τε, -ᾱσι

prs. ἵστημι — sg. recast as ἕστηκα etc., see below; ἕστα-τον; -μεν, -τε, ἑστᾶσι

prs. λείπω — λέλοιπ-α, -ας, -ε; -ατον; -αμεν, -ατε, λελοιπᾶσι
Note generalization of maj. ph. and stem-extension -α (this from endings of sg. 1, pl. 3) sg. 2 -σ after most present and aorist forms.

prs. δίδωμι — δέδω-κα, -κας, -κε; -κατον; -καμεν, -κατε, -κᾱσι

Pluperfect Active

pf. οἶδα — ᾔδ-η/-ειν, -σθα, -ει(ν); ᾖσ-τον, ᾔσ-την; ᾖσ-μεν, -τε, -αν/ᾔδεσαν
Note disguised augment in ᾔ-.

pf. λέλοιπα — ἐλελοίπ-η, -ης, -ει(ν); -ετον, -έτην; -εμεν, -ετε, -εσαν

pf. δέδωκα — ἐδεδώκη etc., as ἑστήκη q.v.

pf. ἕστηκα — ἑστή-κη/εἱστή-κη, ἑστή-κης, -κει(ν); -κετον, -κέτην; -κεμεν, -κετε, -κεσαν

Perfect Mediopassive

pf. δέδωκα — δέδο-μαι, -σαι, -ται; -σθον; -μεσθε, -σθε, -νται
So essentially all others, as ἕσταμαι, τέθειμαι etc. To illustrate cluster developments note also *λελειπ-μαι > λέλειμ-μαι, λέλειψαι, λέλειπται; λελέιφθον; λελείμμεθα, λέλειφθε in pf. med. stems with stem-final consonant, the pl. 3 is periphrastically expressed as λελειμ-μένοι εἰσι (m.).

Pluperfect Mediopassive

pf. δέδωκα — ἐδεδό-μην, -σο, -το; du. 2 -σθον, du. 3 -σθην; -μεθα, -σθε, -ντο
So essentially all others, as ἐλελείμ-μην etc. (same cluster developments as in pf. λέλειμ-μαι); periphrastic pl. 3 (m.) λελειμμένοι ἦσαν.

Future Perfect Middle

pf. λέλοιπα λελείψο-μαι, as fut. passive φανήσομαι above.

Future Active

prs. δίδωμι δώσω, etc., as prs. λείπω above.
prs. φαίνω φανῶ, φανεῖς, etc., as prs. φιλέω > φιλῶ.
prs. ἐλαύνω ἐλῶ, ἐλᾷς, etc., as prs. τῑμάω > τῑμῶ above.

Future middle

prs. λείπω λείψο-μαι, λείψῃ/λείψει, as fut. pass. φανήσομαι above.

Mood Formation

Greek forms imperatives (in part old injunctives, in part recastings of injunctives, but without stem alteration), optatives (with stem extension), and subjunctives (with stem-final alteration) in presents, aorists and perfects; in the future only optatives are formed.

Imperative. Broadly speaking, athematic stems use the minor phase, but there are exceptions, as prs. ἐσ-, 2μι aor. γνω-, στη-, etc. Thematics show the normal stem-final ε/ο distributed as in the imperfect indicative, etc. First aorists have stem-final -σα but σ- before sg. 2 -ον, and both second and first perfects are adjusted to the thematic type. Endings: sg. 2 (athematics) prevailingly -θι, as φάθι/φαθί, ἴ-θι, ἴσ-θι 'be thou' (ι- unclear), 2μι aor. στῆθι, γνῶθι, δῦθι, etc., 2 aor. pass. φανή-θι (1 aor. pass. δόθη-τι by aspirate dissimilation, Grasmann's Law in reverse order), etc., pf. ἴσ-θι 'know thou'; but note its absence in endingless prs. ἵστη, δίδου, δείκνυ etc.; whether these are a true major phase or have been analogically contracted with thematic endingless sg. 2 -ε is uncertain; note also old injunctive *-s* imperatively used in 2μι aorists θέ-ς, δό-ς, ἕ-ς (as also unexpectedly in them. 2 aor. σχές), and 1 aor. -ον (!) < IE *-om*, a verbal noun or infinitive imperatively used(?); (thematics) endingless prs. λεῖπε, 2 aor. λίπε (but with retention of IE accentual type in λαβέ and a few others), and analogically, 2 pf. λέλοιπε, 1 pf. δέδωκε; in the other persons and numbers, athematics and thematics use the same endings. sg. 3 -τω < IE **tōd*, cf. Skt. *-tāt*, but restricted in Greek to sg. 3, possibly syntactically influenced by lost IE *-tu*, as φά-τω, ἔσ-τω, θέ-τω, φανή-τω, λιπέ-τω, λελοιπέ-τω, δεδωκέ-τω, etc. du. 2 -τον < IE *-tom*, the old injunctive ending throughout. du. 3 -των probably recast after sg. 3 -τω, pl. 3 -ντων from expected -την < IE *-tām*, as in the imperfect indicative, etc. pl. 2 -τε throughout, the old injunctive ending, cf. Hit. extended *-te-n*, Skt. *-ta*, frequently extended to *-tana*. pl. 3, earlier -ντω (by conflation of sg. 3 -τω and lost IE pl. 3 *-ntu*) persisting in some other dialects, but in Attic extended to -ντων from imperfect indicative etc. Alternatively, the sg. 3 may be extended by -σαν to form a pl. 3, this, of course, from 1 aorist pl. 3.

prs. athem. sg. 2 ἴ-θι, ἴ-τω; du. 2 ἴ-τον, ἴ-των; pl. 2 ἴ-τε, ἰ-όντων (thematic!)/ἴ-τω-σαν
them. λεῖπε (2 aor. λίπε), λειπέ-τω; -τον, -των; λειπό-ντων/λειπέ-τω-σαν
pf. λέλοιπε, λελοιπέ-τω; -τον, -των; -τε, λελοιπό-ντων
1 aor. τίμησ-ον, -α-τω; -α-τον, -α-των; -α-τε, -α-ντων

Optative. Stems historically athematic add mood marker -ιη/ῑ for the most part to their minor phase, as φᾰ-ιη-, ἱστα-ιη-; there are exceptions, as *ἐ(σ)-ιη-, 2μ pf. εἰδε(σ)-ιη- for expected *ιδ-ι̯η- etc. Stems historically thematic add marker -ι to stem-final -ο, as λειπο-ι- and some historical athematics have gone over to this pattern, as ιο-ι-, δεικνυο-ι; first aorist stems have been recast to a partially thematic pattern, stem-final -σα-ι- but alternatively -σεια- (obscure) in certain persons. The mood marker -ιη/ῑ- is historically biphasal, with the usual distribution, sg. -ιη-, du. and pl. -ῑ-, but -ιη- occurs increasingly in the du. and pl. in prose, while -ῑ- tends to become a poetic archaism. When -ιη- occurs in cluster with preceding σ- (itself then lost), as sg. 1 *ἐσ-ιη-ν > εἴην the retention of ι is phonological; when intervocalic, as φαίην, it is analogical. Endings: sg. 1, -ν for athematics, -μι (!) for thematics and first aorists (cf. below); sg. 2 and pl. 2, the usual secondary endings; pl. 3, secondary -εν < IE *-ent*, perhaps originally throughout, but replaced in athematics by -σαν (from first aorist pl. 3) whenever preceded by -ιη. In thematics, both theoretical sg. 1 *-*oi̯-m̥* and pl. 3 *-*oi̯-n̥t* would > -οια (actually cited as a sg. form from Arcadian); the ambiguity is avoided by the Attic analogical substitutes -οι-μι, -οι-εν.

prs. athem.	φαίη-ν, -ς, φαίη; ---, ---; φαῖ-μεν/φαίη-μεν, φαῖ-τε/-η-τε, φαῖ-εν/-η-σα, εἴη-ν, -ς, εἴη; εῖ-τον/-η-τον, -την; -μεν, -τε, εῖ-εν/εἴη-σαν, ἱσταίη-ν, διδοίη-ν, τιθεί- etc., similarly.
them.	λείποι-μι, -ς, λείποι; -τον, -την; -μεν, -τε, λείποι-εν. Similarly historically athematic ἴοι-μι (but this also allows conflated sg. 1 ἰοίη-ν), δεικνύοι-μι etc. Strangely, contracts may be regularly formed, or follow an athematic model, sg. 1 τῑμῷ-μι, φιλοῖ-μι, δηλοῖ-μι etc.
aor. athem.	σταίη-ν, δοίη-ν, θείη-ν, etc. them. λίποι-μι, etc., as prs. λείποιμι above; 1 aor. τιμήσαι-μι, -ς/-σειας, -σαι/-σειε; -σαι-τον, -την; -μεν, -τε, εν/-σεια
aor. pass. 2	φανησοί-μην, -ο, -το; -σθον, -σθην; -μεθα, -σθε, -ντο. Similarly aor. pass. 1 δοθησοί-μην
2 pf.	ἐσταίη-ν, etc.
2 pf.	(as if thematic) λελοίποι-μι etc., and 1 pf. δεδώκοι-μι etc., (both as if thematic) as prs. λείποιμι above.
fut. pf.	λελείψοι-μι etc., as prs. λείποιμι above.
fut.	δώσοι-μι etc.

Subjunctive. In IE proper, according to the theory set forth in **39**, ambiguity between the factual and modal use of injunctives was eventually removed, when their modal use was to be made unmistakable, by an exchange of stem finals: historically athematic stems extended their major phase by the thematic stem-final *-e/-o*; historically thematic stems altered their stem final to that of the (ultimately, at least) monophasal aorist stems in quasi-suffixal *-e* or *-a*, thus creating a new mood, the 'subjunctive.' In even the earliest Greek the type in *-e/-o* ('short-vowel subjunctive') is dying out, though it persists somewhat vestigially in Homeric Greek, chiefly in the pl. 1, 2 of first aorists, as pl. 2 ἀλγήσ-ε-τε and seems to survive, disguised by contraction, in some Attic forms to historically athematic stems. In the Greek development of the other type, it is only subjunctive stems in *-ē* that are involved; this stem final was differentiated into -η/-ω after the pattern of thematics, and with the same apportionment, i.e., -η in sg. 2, 3, du. 2, 3, and pl. 2, -ω in sg. 1, pl. 1

and 3, and it is this type which ultimately becomes universal. Endings: Greek, like Sanskrit, implies some late IE proper vacillation between primary and secondary endings; if the earliest subjunctives were formed only to aorist stems (as some forms in OLat., OIr., and Toch. may imply), the secondaries may once have been used exclusively, but this is no longer the case in even the earliest Sanskrit and Greek; in Hom. Greek typically 'athematic' primary endings are sometimes used in the sg., as sg. 1 ἐθέλω-μι, ἐθέλῃ-σθα, ἐθέλῃ-σι. The ultimate Attic series of stem final plus endings is: sg. 1 -ω, -ῃ-ς, -ῃ (in the sg. 2, 3 earlier -η has been altered to -ῃ to match -ει in themat. prs. -ει-ς, -ει though this orthography may be a mere scribal convention with no phonological justification), du. 2, 3 -η-τον; pl. 1 -ωμεν, -ητε, -ωσι, all of course somewhat disguised when a contraction is involved.

prs. athem.	φῶ, φῃ-ς, φῃ; φῆ-τον; φῶ-μεν, φῆ-τε, φῶ-σι
	ἴω, ἴῃ-ς, ἴῃ; ἴη-τον; ἴω-μεν, ἴη-τε, ἴω-σι
	ὦ, ᾖ-ς, ᾖ; ἦ-τον; ὦ-μεν, ἦ-τε, ὦ-σι
	*ἱστά-ω > ἱστῶ, *τιθέ-ω > τιθῶ; both as φῶ above.
	*διδό-ω > διδῶ, -ς, διδῶ; -τον; -μεν, -τε, -σι.
prs. them.	λείπω, λείπῃ-ς, λείπῃ; -τον; λείπω-μεν, λείπη-τε, λείπω-σι.
	So also (analogically) δεικνῦω.
aor. athem.	στῶ, θῶ as prs. φῶ above; δῶ as prs. διδῶ above. But analogically them. δύω etc.
1 aor.	τῑμήσω, etc., as prs. λείπω.
2 aor.	λίπω, etc., as prs. λείπω.
2μ pf.	ἑστῶ, etc., as prs. φῶ; γνῶ, etc., as prs. διδῶ.
1, 2 pf.	δεδώκω, etc., λελοίπω etc., as prs. λείπω.

Latin. Two stem systems: present and perfect (the latter a conflation of IE perfects and aorists that had become functionally interchangeable, and a probable Latin neologism). OLat. has vestiges of a distinct *s*- future stem (as sg. 1 *capsō, faxō*: prs. *capiō, faciō*) and of a distinct subjunctive stem (as sg. 3 *-venat*, probably a modally used injunctive of a quasi-suffixal *ā*- aorist : prs. sg. 1 *veniō*; the CL present subjunctive is adapted to the present stem, as sg. 3 *-veniat*). All the CL futures belong to the present system, all CL subjunctives to the present and perfect systems. Latin subjunctives are based partly on IE subjunctives, partly on aorists. Present stems are mostly thematic, some athematics having been adapted to the thematic pattern, though this itself has been somewhat redifferentiated into various types by certain vowel contractions, etc. A few verbs of Conjugations IIIb and IV (see below) may be IE half-thematics (**6**). Examples (often with considerable alteration) of various IE present-stem types occur in the Table of Principal Parts below, where, however, the first basis of classification is the traditional descriptive one by 'conjugations' involving the redifferentiations noted above, whereby some earlier distinct IE types come to be descriptively identical, as in sg. 2 athem. **-ā-s* (no. 2) and themat. **-ā-i̯e-s* (no. 19) both > Lat. *-ās*. The presence or absence of particular present-stem formants does not particularly enter into the classification by conjugations except where it involves the eventual stem-final vowel. The conjugations are recognizable from the following endings:

	I	II	IIIa	IIIb	IV
prs. ind. sg. 1 act.	-ō	-eō	-ō	-iō	
2 ,,	-ās	-ēs	-is		-īs
infinitive ,,	-āre	-ēre	-ere		-īre

This classification ignores the different types of perfect stems. The present system includes the present indicative, the neological imperfect indicative (**12**, a probable one-time verbal noun eventually adapted to or replaced by the descriptive present stem + IE root aorist sg. 1 **bhu̯ā-m*, etc., > CL *-ba-m*, etc.), the CL future indicative (a neological coalesced periphrasis in conjugations I, II, a recategorized present subjunctive in IIIa, b, IV), the present and 'future' imperative (the latter a recategorization of certain present imperative forms, partly analogical), the CL present subjunctive (apparently based on IE aorist injunctives with stem final *-ē* and *-ā*, but variously distributed and ultimately adapted to the present stem, as in OLat. *-venat* > CL *-veniat* above; there are also some recategorized 'short-vowel' subjunctives, i.e., the future perfect indicatives of the regular conjugations, and the future of *sum*), the 'imperfect subjunctive' (recategorized from certain IE *s*-aorist subjunctives, but morphologically adapted to the present system). All these are inflected in both the active and the passive. Perfect stems are descriptively of four (or five) types: (1) reduplicating, mostly IE perfects, but a few reduplicated aorists (as **tetag-* > *tetig-*, cf. Gk. aor. ptc. τετάγων); (2) without formant (some earlier reduplicated perfects that have lost reduplication by haplology in preverbal compounds, etc.), others lengthened grade aorists, inherited or analogical, as pf. *lēg-* : prs. *lĕgō*; (3) IE *s*- aorists, inherited or analogical; (4 and 5) probably neological *u*- and *v*- suffixal perfects (but cf. the types Skt. pf. *jajñau*, OE prt. *cnēow*, WToch. prt. sg. 1 *prekwa*). More conservatively, this Latin type may have spread from OLat. sg. 1 *fuvei*, etc., (*-uv-* for antevocalic *-ū-*) a suppletive perfect to prs. *sum*, and itself of Latin type (2). The Latin *-u-* and *-v-* types are mere phonological-orthographic variants. In many verbs of conjugations I and IV the *v*-perfect is virtually a derivative category from the present stem. There is no trace of old phase distribution, the actual CL vocalism sometimes generalizing the old major phase (so **leloi̯q*^{u}*-*, cf. Gk. λέλοιπα with loss of reduplication > Lat. *līq*^{u}*-*, sometimes the old minor phase (so **tutud-*, cf. Skt. pl. 1 *tutudima* : Lat. prs. *tundō*). Note also that differences of stem-internal vocalism between present and perfect are not always due to IE ablaut, but sometimes to later causes, so prs. *tangō* : (aor. >) pf. **tetag-* > *tetig-*, and conversely, identities may be due to later fallings together of vocalisms earlier distinct. Broadly speaking, the concurrent perfect to a present of any conjugation may belong unpredictably to any of the five types, except that there are no *s*- perfects to presents of conjugation I. All perfect stems are extended by *-is-* (of aorist origin) in the sg. 2, pl. 2, and partly in the pl. 3. The perfect system includes the perfect indicative and the following neo-categories, all using the same extended form of the stem: pluperfect indicative (a recategorized **-is-ā-* aorist); future perfect indicative (a recategorized thematic **-is-e-* aorist subjunctive); perfect subjunctive (a recategorized **-is-ī-* aorist optative, and note generalization of the major phase of the optative marker *-ī-*); pluperfect subjunctive (a recategorized *-is-s-ē-* aorist subjunctive, note the threefold repetition of the *s-* aorist marker in e.g., sg. 1 *scrīps-is-s-e-m*); vestigial perfect imperative forms, as sg. 2, 3 *mementō*. All forms of the perfect system are inflected in the active only; their functional equivalents in the passive are periphrastically suppleted.

Typical Principal Parts

Roman numerals indicate the Latin conjugations; Arabic numerals in parentheses indicate apparent **13** stem classes; Arabic numerals before the perfects represent the Latin type class perfects.

	Present sg. 1		Present sg. 2		infinitive	Perfect sg. 1
I	stō	(18)	stās		stāre	1 stetī
	iuvō	(?)	iuvās		iuvāre	2 iūvī
	secō	(2?)		Similarly		4 secuī
	amō	(?)		,,		5 amāvī
	nō	(1)		,,		5 nāvī
	clīno	(5)		,,		5 clīnāvī
	cūrō	(19)		,,		5 curāvī
II	mordeō	(20)	mordēs		mordēre	1 momordī
	sedeō	(20)	sedēs		sedēre	2 sēdī
	videō	(20)		Similarly		2 vīdī
	maneō	(20)	manēs		manēre	3 mānsī
	torqueō	(2)		Similarly		3 torsī
	pateō	(20)		,,		4 patuī
	habeō	(20)		,,		4 habuī
	moneō	(25)		,,		4 monuī
	fleō	(18)		,,		5 flēvī
	pleō	(18)		,,		5 plēvī
IIIa	canō	(8)	canis		canere	1 cecinī
	tangō	(10)	tangis		tangere	1 tetigī
	tendō	(15, 16)		Similarly		tetendī
	pōscō	(12)		,,		1 poposcī
	agō	(8)		,,		2 ēgī
	linquō	(10)		,,		2 līquī
	frangō	(10)		,,		2 frēgī
	dīcō	(8)		,,		3 dīxī
	dūcō	(8)		,,		3 dūxī
	vehō	(8)		,,		3 vēxī
	iungō	(10)		,,		3 iunxī
	temnō	(11)		,,		3 -tempsī
	pectō	(14)		,,		3 pexī

	Present				Perfect
	sg. 1		sg. 2	infinitive	sg. 1
	vīvō	(17)	,,		3 vīxī
	metō	(8)	,,		4 metuī
	gignō	(9)	,,		4 genuī
	metuō	(22)	,,		4 metuī
	serō	(9)	,,		5 sēvī
	sternō	(9)	,,		5 strāvī
	terō	(8)	,,		5 trīvī
	petō	(8)	,,		5 petīvī
	rudō	(8)	,,		5 rudīvī
IIIb	pariō	(18?)	paris	parere	1 peperī
	capiō		Similarly		2 cēpī
	faciō		,,		2 fēcī
	fodiō		,,		2 fōdī
	speciō		,,		3 spēxī
	rapiō		,,		4 rapuī
	sapiō		,,		5 sapīvī (later 4 sapuī)
IV	re-periō	(18?)	-perīs	-perīre	1 -pperī
	veniō		venīs	venīre	2 vēnī
	hauriō		Similarly		3 hausī
	saliō		,,		4 saluī
	audiō		,,		5 audīvī
	fīniō	(21)	,,		5 fīnīvī

Selective Paradigms, active only

prs. ind.	I	amō, amās, amat; amāmus, amātis, amant
	II	moneō, monēs, monet; monēmus, monētis, monent
	IIIa	dūcō, dūcis, dūcit; dūcimus, dūcitis, dūcunt
	IIIb	pariō, paris, parit; parimus, paritis, pariunt
	IV	veniō, venis, venit; venīmus, venītis, veniunt
ipf. ind.	I	amābam, amābās, amābat; amabāmus, amabātis, amābant
	II	monēbām, etc., IIIa dūcēbam, IIIb pariēbam, IV veniēbam, etc.
fut. ind.	I	amābō, amābis, amābit; amābimus, amābitis, amābunt
	II	monēbō, etc.
	IIIa	dūcam, dūcēs, dūcet; dūcēmus, dūcētis, dūcunt
	IIIb	pariam, pariēs, etc. IV veniam, veniēs, etc.
Prs. subj.	I	amem, amēs, amet; amēmus, amētis, ament
	II	moneam, moneās, moneat; moneāmus, moneātis, moneant
	IIIa	dūcam, dūcās, etc. IIIb pariam, pariās, etc. IV veniam, veniās, etc.

ipf. subj.	I	amārem, amārēs, amāret; amārēmus, amārētis, amārent
	II	monērem, monērēs, etc., IIIa dūcerem, etc. IIIb parerem, etc., IV venīrem, etc.
pf. ind.	(1)	peperī, peperistī, peperit; peperimus, peperistis, peperēre/-erunt/-ērunt
	(2)	vēnī, etc. (3) dūxī, etc. (4) monuī, etc. (5) amāvī, etc.
plpf. ind.	(1)	peperer-am, ās, -at; -āmus, -ātis, -ant
	(2)	vēneram, etc. (3) dūxeram, etc. (4) monueram, etc. (5) amāveram, etc.
fut. pf. ind.	(1)	peper-erō, -eris, -erit; -erimus, -eritis, -erint
	(2)	vēnerō, etc.
pf. subj.	(1)	peper-erim, -erīs, -erit; -erīmus, -erītis, -erint
	(2)	vēnerim, etc.
plpf. subj.	(1)	peper-issem, -issēs, -isset; -issēmus, -issētis, -issent
	(2)	vēnissem, etc.
prs. ipv.	I	sg. 2 amā; pl. 2 amā-te. II monē, monēte. IIIa dūc (for exp. *dūce, as vehe), dūcite. IIIb pare, parite. IV vēnī, vēnīte
'fut.' ipv.	I	sg. 2, 3 amātō; pl. 2 amātōte, pl. 3 amantō. II monētō; monētōte, monentō. IIIa dūcitō; dūcitōte, ducuntō. IIIb paritō; paritōte, pariuntō. IV vēnītō; vēnitōte, vēniuntō.

The present system of the verb 'to be' is irregular and is presented here.

prs. ind.	su-m, es, es-t; su-mus, es-tis, su-nt
ipf. ind.	era-m, erā-s, era-t; erā-mus, erā-tis, era-nt
fut. ind.	erō, eri-s, eri-t; eri-mus, eri-tis, eru-nt
prs. subj.	OLat. sie-m, siēs, sie-t (but CL si-m, sī-s, si-t); sī-mus, sī-tis, OLat. sie-nt/CL si-nt. ipf. subj. esse-m, essē-s, etc.

Pl. 3 **senti*, inj. **s-ent* developed a qualitative ablaut variant **s-ont(i)*, cf. OCS *s-ǫtь*, the thematic appearance of which evoked Lat. sg. 1 *su-m*, pl. 1 *su-mus*. Imperfect, apparently a quasi-suffixal *ā-* aorist (!) to maj. ph. *es*. Future, apparently a normal short-vowel subjunctive (cf. Skt. *asa-t*, etc.) to maj. ph. *es-*. Present subjunctive, in its OLat. forms, a biphasal optative to min. ph. *s-*; in CL the min. ph of the mood marker replaces the major (otherwise Sanskrit). Imperfect subjunctive, a neological *s-* aorist *e-* subjunctive built to maj. ph. *es-*. The suppletive perfect system (*fu-ī*, etc.) is completely regular and is probably built to IE aor. **bhū-*.

In spite of the obviously close relationship between Latin and the p-Italic languages (Oscan, Umbrian, etc.) texts of the latter are scanty and verb forms so few, that precise equations of categories can scarcely be made, not only between these languages as a group and Latin, but even among the p-Italic languages themselves. It is probable that there were the same two stem systems as in Latin, but whether the traditional descriptive four conjugational classification of present stems is valid for p-Italic also is questionable. Several morphological differences, however, can be noted. Thus, in the present system, a thematic *se-* future (cf. OLat. *capsō, faxō*) is generalized, even in the verb 'to be', as Osc.,

Umb. *fust.*—The perfect stems differ quite sharply: a. There are no *s-* perfects (cf. Lat. *dūxit* above), nor any in *-u-/-v-*, nor the *-is-* extensions which bulk so large in Latin; b. Stems in *-f-*, as Osc. sg. 3 *aíkdafed,* presumably a coalesced periphrastic with IE thematicized aorist **-bhu̯om, -bhu̯es, -bhu̯et,* etc., as auxiliary; c. Stems in *-t(t)-*, *-l-*, and **-nki̯-*, as Osc. sg. 3 *prúfatted* (based on IE *-to-* participle?), Umb. fut. pf. act. sg. 3 *entelust, purdinšiust* (both perhaps semi-coalesced periphrastics in which a participle or verbal adjective took auxiliary sg. 3 *est,* etc.). A further sharp difference from Latin is that at least in some categories *r-* impersonals or passives may be formed directly (i.e., not periphrastically) from perfect as well as present stems. as Osc. pf. subj. pass. sg. 3 *lamatir,* but Lat. periphrastic *caesus sit.*

Gothic. Three (or two) stem systems: present, preterite singular, preterite dual and plural (but in many case the preterite singular, dual, and plural have the same stem). The over-all classification uses the terms 'strong' and 'weak' in a special sense: strong verbs are those whose preterite stems show (1) stem-internal ablaut change from that of their concurrent presents, (2) reduplication, or (3) both; weak verbs have a preterite stem extended from the present stem by a dental quasi-suffix, in origin perhaps a coalesced auxiliary. The two classes are best treated separately.

Strong verbs. All strong present stems are thematic; a classification of these by IE stem types (**13**) would not be practical, since most old present formants have been extended to the non-present stems as well (for a few exceptions, see Table of Principal Parts, below), so that most strong presents can be treated as IE type **13**, 8. On the basis of stem-internal vocalism (in relation to that of concurrent preterites), reduplication, etc., seven strong classes are recognized (presents mostly of type A; a few, and all of VII 1-3, of type B, see below). The present system includes the present indicative, imperative, and optative, all but the imperative inflected in both the active and passive. Strong preterite stems derive from IE redupl. *o*-grade perfects (*ō-* in the case of heavy bases), non *-s-* aorists (the *s-* aorist does not occur at all in Germanic), or a conflation of both (for these two IE tenses had become functionally interchangeable in Germanic, as also in Italic, Celtic, Tocharian). In class VII (cf. below) the preterite stems are IE redupl. perfects throughout; in its sub-classes VII, 1-3, the identity of stem-internal vocalism in sg. and pl. is phonological (IE maj. ph. **kekōid-*, and min. ph. **kekəid-* from a heavy base, both > *haíhait-*); in VII, 5 and 6 it is analogical (e.g., maj. ph. *laílōt-* being used not only in the sg., but also [for expected min. ph. IE **leləd-* > Goth. **laílat-*. in the dual and plural]). Incidentally, the Goth. reduplicatory *aí* must have spread from instances where it was followed by Goth. *-h, -ƕ*, or *-r*; elsewhere IE *e* would have >Goth. *i*. In the pl. of classes IV and V, and in VI throughout, the preterite stems are IE athematic lengthened-grade aorists (as IE **gu̯ēm-*, Goth. *qēm-*; any possible earlier phase distinction has been levelled out in favor of the major phase. In classes I-III the preterite pl. stems are IE zero-grade thematic aorists (as pre-Goth. pl. 1 **gripa-m*) conflated with min. ph. perfect plurals (as pre-Goth. pl. 1 **gegrip-um*) because of identical stem-internal vocalism; in the conflation the perfect forms lost their reduplication, but their athematic endings prevailed, hence Goth. pl. 1 *-um*, pl. 3 *-un* (and analogically pl. 2 *-uþ*), not **-a-m, *-i-þ, *-a-n*. Finally, in the sg. of classes I-V the stems are IE redupl. *o-* grade maj. ph. perfects (as pre-Goth. sg. 1, 3

**gegraip*) that have lost reduplication through paradigmatic association with unredupl. plurals, hence Goth. *graip*, etc. The preterite system includes the preterite indicative and optative (this latter always formed throughout from the preterite plural stem, where there is any difference), inflected only in the active.

Weak verbs. Stems are of four classes, generally termed 'Weak I, II, III IV', but here listed simply as VIII (which has some subdivisions), IX, X, XI. Stems of VIII are in the main of IE type **13**, 18, though when IE stem-final *-i̯e* (which becomes Goth. *-ji* when preceded by a metrically short monosyllable) is preceded by a metrically long monosyllable or dissyllable, it > *-ei* (Goth. orthography for *ī*), as sg. 2 *nasjis* : *sōkeis*; it is not clear whether Goth. *-ei* in this position is wholly the result of pre-Gothic contraction, or whether it is somehow connected with IE half-thematics in *-ī*. Stems of IX seem to be IE dissyllabic athematics with quasi-suffixal *-ā*, though possibly contractions of type **13**, 19 **-ā-i̯e-* > **ā* > Goth. *ō* are involved. Similarly, stems of X may be such athematics with quasi-suffixal *-ē*, or contractions of types **-ē-i̯e-* > *-ē* (Gothic orthography *ai*) but partly replaced by the thematic pattern, as sg. 1 *-a*, pl. 1 *-am*, pl. 3 *-and*. Finally, though stems of XI appear to be of type **13**, 11, it is likely, since their concurrent preterite stems are built from stem-final *-nō-*, that they are adaptations of type **13**,5 to the normal thematic pattern. Weak preterite stems involve a dental extension discussed in **14**e, and may once have been neological imperfects (formed with a coalesced auxiliary) that had also become functionally interchangeable with aorists and perfects. Note that the extension is preceded, in stems of VIII by *i-* (weak grade of *i̯e*?), in IX by *ō-*, in X by *ai-*, and in XI by *nō-*.

Typical Principal Parts

It is conventional to typify the present stem by the infinitive in *-an* (IX, *-ōn*) rather than by the sg. 1 in *-a* (IX, *-ō*), and the preterite stem(s) by the sg. 1, 3 and pl. 1 respectively

	Prs. infinitive	Prt. sg. 1, 3	Prt. pl. 1
I	greipan	graip	gripum
II	biudan	bauþ	budum
	lūkan (B)	lauk	lukum
III	bindan	band	bundum
IV	baíran	bar	bērum
	qiman	qam	qēmum
V	sitan	sat	sētum
	(wisan)	was	wēsum
	fraíhnan (11)	frah	frēhum
VI	sakan	sōk	-um
	standan	stōþ	-um
VII1	haitan (B)	haíhait	-um
2	stautan (B)	staístaut	-um
3	haldan (B)	haíhald	-um
5	lētan	laíflōt	-um
6	flōkan	faíflōk	-um

	Prs. infinitive	Prt. sg. 1, 3	Prt. pl. 1
VIII	nasjan	nasi-da	-dēdum
IX	salbōn	salbō-da	-dēdum
X	haban	habai-da	-dēdum
XI	fullnan	fullnō-da	-dēdum

The suppletive prs. to prt. *was*, etc., is IE **es-mi*, etc. (**13**, 1) > Goth. sg. *im, is, ist*; pl. *sijum, sijuþ* (these two forms analogically somewhat altered), *sind*.

Select Paradigms

Prs. ind.	
I-VII	sg. greip-a, -is, -iþ; du. 1 -ōs, du. 2 -ats; pl. -am, -iþ, -and
VIII	nasj-a, -is, -iþ; -ōs, -ats; -am, -iþ, -and
	sōk-ja, -eis, -eiþ; -jōs, -jats; -jam, -eiþ, -jand
IX	salbō, -s, -þ; , -s, -ts; -m, -þ, -nd
X	hab-a, -ais, -aiþ; -ōs, ----; -am, -aiþ, -and
XI	fullna, as greipa
Imperative	
I-VII	sg. 2 greip, sg. 3 -adau; du. 2 -ats; pl. 1 -am, 2 -iþ, 3 -andau
VIII	nas-ei, -jadau; -jats; -jam, -jiþ, -jandau
	sōk-ei, -jadau; -jats; -jam, -eiþ, -jandau
IX	salbō, -dau; -ts; -m, -þ, -ndau
X	hab-ai, unattested in sg. 3 and du.; -am, -aiþ, -aindau
XI	fulln, as greip
Opt.	
I-VII	greip-au, -ais, -ai; -aiwa, -aits; -aima, -aiþ, -aina
VIII	nasjau, etc., as greipau
IX	salbō, -s, salbō; -wa, -ts; -ma, -þ, -na
X, XI	habau, fullnau, etc., as greipau
Prt. ind.	
I-VI	graip, graipt, graip; grip-u, -ts; -um, -uþ, -un
VII	haíhait, *haíhait-t > haíhai-st, -t; haíhait-u, etc., as graip
VIII	nasi-da, -dēs, -da; -dēdu, -dēduts; -dēdum, -dēduþ, -dēdun
IX-XI	salbōda, habai-da, fullnō-da, etc.
Prt. opt.	
I-VI	grip-jau, -eis, -i; -eiwa, -eits; -eima, -eiþ, -eina
VII	haíhait-jau, etc., as grip-jau
VIII-XI	nasi-dēdjau, salbō-dēdjau, habai-dēdjau, fullnō-dēdjau, etc.

The verb system and categories of the other old Germanic languages are roughly similar to those of Gothic. In class VII, however, the other languages have for the most part preterites based on IE lengthened-grade aorists (as IE **kēi̯d-* > OE *hēt*, OHG *hiaȥ*, as against pf. **kekōi̯da* > Goth. *haíhait*). But a number of these languages have a few isolated (and frequently much altered) forms based, like those of Gothic, on IE reduplicated perfects (as Northumbrian OE dial. *heht*, beside normal OE *hēt*).

Old Irish. Five stem systems: present, preterite, subjunctive, future (often related to the subjunctive), and preterite passive (this last based on an IE non-finite category, the passive participle in *-to-*, etc.). Thurneysen distinguishes 'strong' verbs, whose non-present stems often differ unpredictably from their presents, and 'weak' verbs, whose non-present categories are normally built by predictable extensions from the present (really general) stem. Weak and strong verbs are conveniently recognized as such from the prs. sg. 3 when formed with the secondary ending IE *-*t* (the 'conjunct' form, cf. below); in weak verbs the preform is *-*ā-t* or *-*ī-t* (long stem-final vowel) > OIr. *-a*, *-i* respectively; in strong verbs it is *-*e-t* (short stem-final vowel), lost in OIr. According to the present-stem types listed in **13**, Thurneysen distinguishes three weak classes, A I-III, and five strong, B I-V. We substitute a continuous numbering: his A I is our I, his B I our IV, his B V our VIII. Morphologically, there are three voices: active, deponent, and passive; but (apart from the preterite passive system) only active forms are treated here. The following orthographical conventions should be noted: an acute accent over a vowel indicates length, not stress; a diaeresis over a vowel shows that it is a separate syllable; any letter written in parentheses in the interior of a word shows, to be sure, that its writing or non-writing is a scribally allowed option, but further (a) if it is a vowel, it is an indication of the vowel-coloring (palatal, neutral, velar) of an adjacent consonant when this would not be automatically inferred from the normally written adjacent vowel, as prs. pl. 3 **bero-nti* > pre-Ir. **bera-nti* > OIr. *ber(a)it*, in which the stem-final vowel > *-i*, but the neutral vowel coloring given to *r-* by its older form *-a* persists, as the optional orthography, *berait*, shows, and (b) in the case of *m(m)* etc., double writing shows that the consonant which might be expected to be lenited is not; a raised dot preceding a verb form shows that it is a 'conjunct' form (i.e., has a secondary ending) and that the following syllable is accented.

Present. Class I, dissyllabic monophasal athematics in *-*ā* (**13**, 2), probably also post-IE contractions of stem-final *-*ā-i̯e-* (19) which have fallen together with them, as sg. 3 **mōrā-ti* > OIr. *mór(a)i-d* (but **mōrā-t* > OIr. *·móra*); Class II, similar athematics in IE *-ē*, contractions of *-*ĕ-i̯e-*, and possibly IE half-thematics in *-ī-*, all giving pre-Ir. sg. 3 *-*ī-ti*, whence OIr. *siri-d* (but *·siri*); Class III, monosyllabic bases with final long vowels (mostly pre-Ir. *-*ī* or *-*ā*) which became secondarily thematic at the expense of hiatus and (to some extent) shortening of preceding vowel, as sg. 3 *rai-d*; Class IV, simple thematics (8), as sg. 3 *beri-d* (but *·beir*), *fedi-d*, *celi-d*, *rethi-d*, *techi-d*, *agi-d*, *cani-d* beside various other originally characterized thematics whose formant has been analogically extended to the whole paradigm, as sg. 3 **pibe-ti* (9) > *ibi-d* (but prt. pl. 3 *ibset*, here from an *s-* aorist), *nasci-d* (12) (but prt. sg. 3 *nenaisc*, here from a reduplicated perfect); Class V, thematics with formant *-i̯e-*, as **gabi̯e-ti* (18) > OIr. *gaibi-d* (*-i-* of the first syllable showing palatal 'coloring' of *b*, due to earlier following *-*i*; in this class there may be some confusion with old half-thematics in *-ī-*); Class VI, thematics with *-n-* infix, as *bongi-d, dingi-d, roindi-d* (10), with pre-stem final consonant in OIr. always *d* or *g*; Class VII, athematics with IE *-nā-/-nə-* suffix (5) (minor phase generalized in OIr.), as **bhinə-ti* > *benai-d* (*-a-* showing 'neutral' coloring of *n-* due to earlier following *-ə*, itself not lost, but altered to *-i*); Class VIII, athematics with IE *-neu-/-nu-* suffix (6), minor phase generalized, as **krenu-t* > *·chrin* (no form with primary ending cited). Classes VII and VIII can be distinguished only by their different umlauting effects on the vocalism of the preceding syllable. Possibly such presents as pre-Ir. **balne-t* (11) should be accounted a separate OIr. class (so apparently Pokorny, Altirische Gramm. Sammlung Göschen, p. 65). Note that because of various phonological changes, etc., the difference between athematic and thematic inflection is no longer apparent in Old Irish. The present system includes the present indicative (in two series, the 'absolute' with primary endings, and the 'conjunct' with secondary endings), the imperfect indicative (origin unclear, conjunct endings only), and, as a rule, the imperative.

Preterite. Active stems (based mostly on IE aorists and perfects, which as in Italic and Germanic had become functionally interchangeable and indistinguishable) are of five types: 1, IE reduplicated perfects, as sg. 3 *bobig, cechain* : prs. *bongi-d, cani-d* (redupl. vowel normally *e*, but with various exceptions for various causes, or phonologically lost or disguised, as with perfectivating preverb *ro-*, sg. 3 *roíchan*). There is no true retention of old phase distribution, but OIr. syncope results in forms like pl. 1 *·cechnammar*, which could easily be mistaken for a historical minor-phase form. IE lengthened grade aorists with stem-internal **-ō-, *-ā-* > OIr. *-á*, while **-ē-* > OIr. *-í*, as sg. 3 *·ráth* (*-i* showing palatal coloring of *-th*, due to lost final vowel) : prs. *rethi-d*, *·fíd* : prs. *fedi-d*. Isolated IE them. aor. **ludhe-t* (cf. Gk. ἤλυθε) > OIr. *luid*, suppletive prt. to prs. *téit*. IE athematic root aorists in sg. 3 *-t*, as **bher-t* > OIr. *bert*; the personal ending has come to be a tense marker used in all persons and numbers, as sg. 1 pre-Ir. **berto* > **birtu* > OIr. *biurt* (*-u-* showing velar quality of the following cluster), cf. the somewhat similar development in MWelsh 'aorist' *can-t* and Goth. prt. *stō-þ*. Strong verbs regularly have preterites belonging to one of these four types, but weak verbs have as preterite a recasting of the IE *s-* aorist, generally built from the present stem and with pre-Ir. tense-marker **-ss-* (the doubling perhaps spread from sg. 3 **-s-t* > *-ss*), this again extended to a thematic in all other persons, hence sg. 3 **karas-t* > **karass* > OIr. *·car*, but pl. 3 **karassant* > OIr. *·carsat*. Two strong verbs, IV *ibi-d* and V *gaibi-d* form *s-* preterites (pl. 3 *ibse-t, gabse-t*).

Subjunctive. Stems are of two classes, *-ā* and *-s*, both based on IE modally used aorist injunctives. *ā-* subjunctives are normal for weak verbs, as sg. 3 *·móra* (identical with corresponding indicative) and occur in certain strong verbs, where for the most part they are obviously no part of the present system, as sg. 3 *·gaba* : prs. ind. *gaibi-d*, *·bía* : prs. ind. *benai-d*; in a few instances, with presents of Class IV, they belong to the present system, as sg. 3 *·bera, ·aga* : prs. *beri-d, agi-d*. *s-* subjunctives are normal for strong verbs with pre-stem final dental, guttural (*a*-subjunctive *aga* just noted is exceptional), or *-nn*. Some *s-* subjunctives (probably the oldest ones) retained the stem-internal long vowel of their remote antecedents, the IE lengthened-grade aorists; others were formed or reformed with the stem-internal vocalism (usually short) of their concurrent presents; in the sg. 3 even these show compensatory lengthening (from loss of final **-ss-t*); in the other persons the pre-Ir. cluster *-*ss*- > OIr. -*s*- for those of lengthened grade origin, but remains -*ss*- for others, hence (to prs. *bongi-d*) prt. sg. 3 **bhōg-s-t* > **bōss-t* > OIr. *bó*, pl. 3 *bósat*, but (to prs. *fedi-d*) prt. sg. 3 **fed-s-t* > **fess-t* > OIr. *fé*, pl. 3 *fessat*. The subjunctive stem also includes a neo-category, the 'imperfect subjunctive', modelled on the imperfect indicative.

Future. Stems (treated here because of the similarity if not actual relationship of the *s*-aorist and the *s*- future) are of two general classes, (a) *s*- (with various subtypes) used in most strong verbs, and (b) *f*- used in weak verbs. The simplest subtype of *s*- future occurs e.g., in sg. 3 **sed-s-ti* (athem.!) > OIr. *seiss* : prs. **sodei̯e-ti* (?) > *saidi-d*. Generally, however, *s*- futures had *i*- reduplication, as sg. 3 **gʷhigʷhed-s-ti* > OIr. *gigis* : prs. V *guidi-d*; often the vocalism of the stem syllable umlauts the redupl. -*i*- to -*e*-, as **mimād-s-ti* > OIr. *memais* : prs. V *maidi-d*. The marker -*s*- is often extended to thematic -*se*- (when this happens, the formation is physically and probably historically identical with that of Sanskrit desideratives of type sg. 3 *bibhitsati*); if thematic -*se*- is preceded by a vowel, the -*s*- itself is lost by lenition, as **kikanāse-ti* > OIr. *cechnai-d* : prs. IV *cani-d* (in this example note the lenition of the second *-*k*- to spirant -*ch*-, and the ultimate loss of the following vowel by syncope), hence such futures are only apparently 'asigmatic.' Finally, the occurrence of a different ablaut grade in the stem syllable, as in **kik̥l̥se-ti* > pre-Ir. **kechla*- precipitated a cluster reduction -*chl*- to -*l*- and consequent compensatory lengthening of redupl. -*e*- to -*é*- (if the cluster had arisen only by normal syncope in late pre-Ir. times, as in *cechnai-d* above, no such reduction would have taken place); the end result is OIr. fut. ·*céla* (with effectively concealed reduplication) : prs. IV *celi-d*. This last subtype spread analogically to many verbs where it could not have arisen phonologically, as fut. *bérai-d* : prs. IV *beri-d*.—The origin of the *f*- future (as sg. 3 *lé*(*i*)*cfi-d* : prs. II *lé*(*i*)*ci-d* is unclear. There are serious phonological difficulties in deriving OIr. -*f*- from IE -*bh*- or -*bhu̯*-, so that the OIr. forms can hardly be connected with the Lat. fut. type *amābō*, *monēbō* (though Pedersen VKG § 457 persists in this view, but cf. Thurneysen, Altirisches Handbuch § 637). The inflection, ultimately at least, follows that of the *ā*- subjunctive.—The future stem system also includes a neo-category, the 'imperfect' or 'conditional' future modelled on the imperfect indicative.

Preterite passive. This is in origin a non-finite form, the IE passive participle in the sg. nom. *-*to-s*, etc., never with expressed auxiliary. In the sg. 3 the masc. is generalized, as IE **bhr̥tos* > pre-Ir. **brita*(*s*) > ·*breth* (the phonological development of the -*t*- is conditioned by neighboring sounds, as in ·*mórad*/*th*, ·*léced*/*th*, ·*nass* : prs. *mórai-d*, *lé*(*i*)*ci-d*, *nasci-d*); in the pl. 3 the IE fem. form is generalized, as IE **bhr̥tās* > OIr. ·*bretha* (similarly, ·*mortha*, ·*leictha*, ·*nassa*).

Absolute and conjunct inflection. As stated in **8**, IE injunctives (with 'secondary' endings), though originally without tense limitation, in many of the continuant languages came to be largely limited to preterite implication once the more specifically presential 'primaries' came into use. In pre-Irish (probably in all old Celtic, since there are traces of the same situation in Middle Welsh q.v.,) a different apportionment of these endings arose, probably at first in the present indicative only. The 'primaries' (in OIr. grammatical terminology, the 'absolute' endings) were used only when there was no preverb (or accentually equivalent preverbal particle, as **nē* 'not' >OIr. *ní*), but with preverbs the secondaries ('conjunct' endings), as sg. 3 **bhere-ti* > *berid*, but **nē bhere-t*, **eks-bhere-t* > *ní·beir*, *as·beir* (though in some archaic texts conjunct endings appear even without preverb or the like). Interestingly, this same apportionment of endings spread from the present indicative to the present subjunctive, the future, and to most types of preterites; the fact that it could spread to preterites shows that the 'primaries' no longer, at least, had any specific connotation of presentiality, as (*s*- prt.) sg. 3 **karas-t* > **karass* > OIr. (conjunct) *·car*, but (prim.) **karas-ti* > **karassi*, > OIr. (absolute) *car(a)is*. On the other hand, much of this spreading may not have taken place until the final sounds of many endings had been lost, or at least so far weakened that differences in the neo-final syllable (vocalism, 'coloring' of a consonant) were all that was left; these relatively slight differences might more readily have lent themselves to the creation of analogical neologisms affording parallels to existing pairs of forms. This expected absolute/conjunct opposition became so far grammaticalized as to be somehow provided for even in the preterite passive, of non-finite origin. Thus, the preterite passive forms described in the preceding paragraph are used as conjunct forms; when a corresponding absolute form is needed, one derived from IE suffixed **-ti̯o-s* is used, as sg. 3 **bhr̥ti̯os* > OIr. *breth(a)e* for expected **brithe* after conjunct *·breth*. In the OIr. neological imperfect indicative, ipf. subjunctive, and ipf. future only conjunct endings are used.

Deuterotonic and prototonic forms of preverbal compounds. In preverbal compounds (all of which take conjunct endings) the stress is regularly on the second element, whether that be a preverb or the verb proper (hence called deuterotonic), and the verb proper suffers little if any alteration from the accentual shifting involved. In certain syntactic situations, however (the simplest perhaps where the negative particle *ní* immediately precedes the verb), the accent rests on the first element of the whole sequence and the verb proper, as well as its preverb(s), suffers such drastic accentual and syllabic reduction, as to make the resultant form almost unrecognizable, e.g., (deut.) *as·beir* 'says' : (proto.) *ní·epir* 'does not say.'

Special relative forms. Some mood-tense categories have special relative forms in the sg. 3, pl. 1, 3, obviously not all of the same origin. In the prs. and fut. sg. 3 the relative form ends in *-s*, the pl. 1, 3 in *-e* as an additional syllable, sometimes entailing syllabic loss in the normal stem-final syllable. For the present active of strong verbs the actual relative forms are here shown below the normal ones:

Normal sg. 3	berid	pl. 1 berm(a)i	pl. 3 ber(a)it
Relative	beres	berm(a)e	bert(a)e

Various explanations have been proposed, cf. the special grammars.

Infixal and suffixal object pronouns with verbs. Abbreviated 'tags' of personal pronouns (functionally either direct or indirect objects) infixed between a preverb and a verb are very common in OIr., as *ro-m·gab* 'he has taken me', *ro-t·bia* 'there will be for thee.' Suffixal pronouns are less common in OIr., but when used may entail syncope, etc., in the verb itself, as sg. 3 *berth-i* 'he bears it', *guidmi-t* 'we pray it.'

Typical Principal Parts (forms sg. 3 except as noted)

	Present	Preterite	Subjunctive	Future	Preterite Pass.
I	ícc-(a)id, ·icca	ícc(a)i-s, ·ícc	ícc(a)i-d, ·icca	íccf(a)i-d, ·íccfa	íccth(a)e
II	siri-d, ·siri	siri-s, ·sir	siri-d, ·sirea	sirfi-d, ·sirfea	sirthe
III	*bá(a)ï-d, ·bá	·beb(a)e	·báa	·beba	———
IV	agi-d, ·aig	·acht	·aga	·ebla (!)	·acht
	beri-d, ·beir	birt, ·bert	·bera	bérai-d, ·béra	·breth
	fedi-d, ·feid	·fíd	·fĕ, pl. 3 fessat	·fé, pl. 3 fessat	·fess
	celi-d, ·ceil	·celt	·cela	·céla	·cleth
	rethi-d, ·reith	·ráith	·ré, pl. 3 ·ressat	·ré, pl. 3 ·ressat	·ress
	techi-d, ·teich	·táich	·té, pl. 3 ·tessat	·té	———
	cani-d, ·cain	·cechuin, -ain	·cana	·cechna	·cét
	ibi-d, ·ib	·ib, pl. ·ibset	·eba	·iba, pl. íb(a)it	·ibed
	nasc(a)id, ·naisc	·nenaisc	·ná, pl. ·nássat	·nena, pl. ·nensat	·nass
V	gaibi-d, ·gaib	·ga(i)b, ·gabsat	·gaba	·géba	·gabad
	gu(i)di-d, ·guid	·gáid	·gé, pl. ·gessat	sg. 1 ·gigius	·gess
	sa(i)di-d, ·said	·sid(?)	seiss	seiss	———
VI	bongi-d, ·boing	bob(a)ig	·bó, pl. ·bósat	·biba, pl. ·bibsat	·bocht
	tongi-d, ·toing	·teth(a)ig	·tó, pl. ·tóssat	·tith, pl. ·titsat	?
VII	benai-d, ·ben	·bí	bíä	·bíä	·bíth
	crenai-d, ·cren	·cíuir	·criä	———	———
VIII	ara ·chrin	·chíuir	·chríä	·chíur(a)i	———
	at ·baill	·balt	·bela	·béla	

Select Paradigms (active forms only; special relative forms not included)

	sg. 1	sg. 2	sg. 3	pl. 1	pl. 2	pl. 3
Prs. I abs.	ícc(a)im(m)	ícc(a)i	ícc(a)id	íccm(a)i	íccth(a)e	íccait
conj.	·ícc(a)im(m)/-u	·ícc(a)i	·ícca	·íccam	·ícc(a)id	·íccat
II abs.	sirim(m)	siri	sirid	sirmi	sirthe	sirit
conj.	·sirim(m)/-(i)u	·siri	·siri	·sirem	·sirid	·siret
IV etc. abs.	biru	biri	berid	berm(a)i	beirthe	ber(a)it
conj.	·biur	·bir	·beir	·beram	·berid	·berat
Ipf. I conj.	·ícc(a)inn	·ícctha	·íccad	·íccm(a)is	·íccth(a)e	·ícct(a)is
II conj.	·sirinn	·sirthea	·sired	·sirmis	·sirthe	·sirtis
IV etc. conj.	·berinn	·beirthea	·bered	·beirmis	·beirthe	·beirtis
Prt. abs. (redup.)	cechan	cechan	cechain, -uin	cechnaimmir	———	cechnaitir
conj.	·cechan	·cechan	·cechain	·cechnammar	·cechn(a)id	·cechnatar
(length.) abs.	gád	gád	gáid	gádaimmir	?	gáda(i)tir
conj.	·gád	·gád	·gáid	·gádammar	·gá(i)did	·gádatar
(t) abs.	?	?	birt	?	?	bertaitir
conj.	·biurt	·birt	·bert	·bertammar	·bertaid	·ber(ta)tar

	sg. 1	sg. 2	sg. 3	pl. 1	pl. 2	pl. 3
(s, I) abs.	íccsu	íccs(a)i	ícc(a)is	íccsaimmi	?	íccs(a)it
conj.	˙íccus	˙ícc(a)is	˙ícc	˙íccsam	˙íccsaid	˙íccsat
(s, II) abs.	sirsiu	sirsi	siris	sirsimmi	?	sirsit
conj.	˙sir(i)us	˙siris	˙sir	˙sirsem	˙sirsid	˙sirset
Subj. abs. (ā, I)	ícca	ícc(a)e	= prs.	= prs.	= prs.	= prs.
conj.	˙ícc	˙ícc(a)e	˙ícca	,,	,,	,,
(ā, II) abs.	sirea	sire	= prs.	,,	,,	,,
conj.	˙sir	˙sire	˙sirea	,,	,,	,,
Ipf. subj. (ā, I, II)	--		= imperfect	--		
Sbj. (s)abs.	?	ge(i)ssi	geiss	gesm(a)i	?	gess(a)it
conj.	˙gess	˙geiss	˙gé	˙gessam	˙gessid	˙gessat
ipf. (s) conj. only	˙ge(i)ssinn	?	˙ge(i)ssed	˙gesm(a)is	?	˙gest(a)is
Fut. (f, I)						
abs.	íccfa	íccf(a)e	íccf(a)id	íccfaimmi	íccfaide	íccfait
conj.	˙íccub	˙íccf(a)e	˙íccfa	˙íccfam	˙íccf(a)id	˙íccfat
(f, II) abs.	sirfea	sirfe	sirfid	sirfimmi	sirfide	sirfit
conj.	˙siriub	˙sirfe	˙sirfea	˙sirfem	˙sirfid	˙sirfet
Ipf. fut. (f; I) conj. only	˙íccf(a)inn	˙íccfada	˙íccfad	˙íccfaimmis	˙íccfaide	˙íccfaitis
(, II) conj. only	˙sirfinn	˙sirfeda	˙sirfed	˙sirfimmis	˙sirfide	˙sirfitis
Fut. (s) abs.	gigsea	gigsi	gigis	gigsimmi	gigest(a)e	gigsit
conj.	˙gig(i)us	˙gigis	˙gig	˙gigsem	˙gigsid	˙gigset
(Ipf. fut.) conj. only	˙gigsinn	?	˙gigsed	˙gigsimmis	?	˙gigsitis
Fut. abs. (redupl.)	cechna	cechn(a)e	cechn(a)id	cechn(a)immi	cechn(a)ithe	cechn(a)it
conj.	˙cechan	˙cechn(a)e	˙cechna	˙cechnam	˙cechn(a)id	˙cechnat
Ipf. fut. redupl. conj. only	˙cechn(a)inn	˙cechnatha	˙cechnad	˙cechn(a)im-mis	˙cechnaithe	˙cechnaitis
Ipv. I		ícc	íccad	íccam	ícc(a)id	íccat
II		sir	sired	sirem	sirid	siret
IV, etc.		beir	berad, -ed	beram	berid	berat

The prs. abs. forms of the verb 'to be'

am	it	is	ammi	adib	it

are of special interest because of the unlenited *m* of the sg. 1 and pl. 1, in both of which *m* represents the IE cluster -*sm*-, hence was so far lengthened and strengthened as to resist lenition. It is probably from these forms that the unlenited sg. 1 *-m* of later Old (and Middle) Irish and the *m* of OIr. conj. pl. 1 forms have spread.

New Welsh. One general stem, since all verbs except a few 'irregulars' have now become weak; a few require slight phonological adjustments. All recognizable present-stem formants, as IE *-sk(e)-* in sg. 1 *archaf*, IE *-nā-/-nə-* in *prynaf*, have been extended to the whole paradigm, as aor. sg. 1 *erchais, prynais*. Preverbs are mostly absorbed into the stem, as **upo-ret-*, **do-u̯et-* in *gwaredaf, dywedaf*, without corresponding simplices. Many present forms, as sg. 1 *-af* < **-ā-mi*, imply a dissyllabic athematic stem in *-ā-/-ə-* (**13**, 2); MW had some in sg. 1 *-if* < **-ē-mi* or half-thematic **-ī-mi*, but some preforms, even in the present indicative, imply a thematic stem final, so that a number of different stem types must have become established at particular points in the pattern that eventually emerged. All non-present categories are now formed in the same way for all verbs (except 'irregulars'). MW (numerous texts) has a paradigm not greatly different, except in a few orthographical details, from that of NW. OW texts are scanty and fragmentary; some scraps of OW text quoted in MW text imply one-time greater paradigmatic complexity, so *trenghit golut ny threingk molut* 'wealth perishes, fame perishes not' implies an opposition of 'absolute' and 'conjunct' endings like that in OIr (some preforms set up for specific paradigmatic points in NW carry the same implication). Presumably there was a good deal of morphological simplification, as well as emergence of some innovations, in p-Celtic times; the ultimately emerging categories and paradigms of Cornish and Breton are roughly similar to those of NW.

Typical New Welsh Paradigm

		impersonal
prs. ind.	sg. 1 caraf sg. 2 ceri, sg. 3 câr; pl. 1 carwn, pl. 2 cerwch, pl. 3 carant;	cerir
ipv.	sg. 2 câr, sg. 3 cared; pl. 1 carwn, pl. 2 cerwch, pl. 3 carent/-ant	carer
subj.	carwyf, cerych, caro; carom, caroch, caront	carer
ipf. ind.	carwn, carit, carai; carem, carech, cerynt/carent	cerid
subj.	carwn, carit, carai; carem, carech, cerynt/carent	cerid
aor. ind.	cerais, ceraist, carodd; carasom, carasoch, carasant	carwyd
plpf. ind.	caraswn, carasit, carasai; carasem, carasech, carasynt/-ent	caresid/carasid

Comment. Stem-internal vowel changes (as *a* : *e* in some forms above) are umlaut due to the vocalism of the following syllable (such vocalism sometimes still extant, sometimes altered or lost). Such changes in NW do not go further back than pre-W or p-Celtic times, never to IE ablaut. As to personal endings, and endingless sg. 3, (as prs. *câr*) these imply generalization of IE secondary *-t*; pl. 3 *-nt*, that of IE primary *-nti* (cf. OIr. conjunct and absolute endings); pl. 1 *-n*, pl. 2 *-ch* where they occur, imply suffixation of initial 'tags' of subject pronouns (NW pl. 1 *ni*, pl. 2 *chwi*), with partial or complete loss of earlier personal ending in cluster development.

Particular categories. Present indicative, complicated analogical changes in pl. 1, 2. Present imperative, sg. 3 *-ed* < themat. sg. 3 med. injunctive **-eto*, but some other forms perhaps partly recast from earlier optatives. Present subjunctive, held to be an IE **se-* future, but can equally be held a thematic short-vowel subjunctive to the *s-* aorist (not sharing the doubling of *s* > *ss* that occurred in all indicative categories of this origin); this single *s* survives in MW as *h* in some forms (so pl. 1 *karhom*), but has lost it in NW. Imperfect indicative, optative of athematic *ā-* stems; for the optative as imperfect, cf. OArm., WToch., and some Skt. forms. Imperfect subjunctive, an analogical 'optative' to the 'single *s* short-vowel subjunctive' described above, cf. sg. 3 MW *karhei*, NW *carai*, generally influenced by the imperfect indicative. Aorist, early functional falling together of IE perfect and aorist leaves a few interesting vestiges in MW, as sg. 3 *cigleu* (an old redupl. pf. like Skt. *suśrava* : prs. *śr̥ṇoti*), *cant* (reformed from an old root aorist sg. 3 like OIr. *·bert* [but whereas OIr. *·bert* seems to be < IE **bhert*!, W. *cant* implies a thematic reformation < **kante-t*]), *gwa-rawt*, *dy-wawt* (old lengthened-grade aorists : prs. NW *gwa-redaf*, *dy-wedaf*; but even in MW the *s-* aorist has all but swept the field, its *s* doubled to *ss* (generalized from sg. 3 **-as-t* > **-as-s* as in OIr.), hence sg. 1 **-assō* (conjunct ending) > q-, p-Celt. **-assu* (whence OIr. *carus*) > pre-W. **-assi* > NW *-ais* (note epenthesis of preceding *-a-* > *-ai-*, with consequent ultimate umlaut of stem-internal vowel in NW *cerais*); the sg. 3 *carodd* has an analogical added ending. The pluperfect indicative is probably a neo-category built to the *s-* aorist (described above) on the analogy of the imperfect. The impersonals in *-r* are of course related to those of Hittite, p-Italic, etc. (OW has forms like *-etor*, in which the impersonal is compounded with a middle ending, as in Hittite, Phrygian, Latin, Tocharian, etc.); those in *-t* may well be related to the Hittite m.p. forms in *-t(i)*.

Armenian. Two stem systems, present and aorist. Present stems are descriptively grouped in four 'conjugations' according to their sg. 1 endings: I *-e-m*, II *-i-m*, III *-a-m*, IV *-u-m* (sometimes arranged in a different order), and an isolated sg. 1 *g-o-m*. Verbs in *-i-m* are regularly passive to actives in *-e-m*, or 'deponents' in their own right. Note that voice distinctions are not implemented by different personal endings, as largely in the majority of the IE continuant languages, but by difference in stem finals; in one category, the imperfect, they are not implemented at all, as ipf. sg. 1 *berei* to both I *berem* and II *berim*. There is no distinction between athematic and thematic presents; if we compare the inflections of what earlier must have been such, we see how a compromise inflectional pattern has emerged e.g., in I sg. 1 *em* 'am' (**13**, 1), *bere-m* (**13**, 8), sg. 2 *e-s*, *bere-s*; pl. 1 *e-mkʿ*, *bere-mkʿ*, pl. 3 *e-n*, *bere-n* essentially follow IE athem. **es-mi*, **es-si*; pl. 1 **(e)s-m-* (analogical məj. ph.), pl. 3 **s-enti*, but the other persons sg. 3 **-e-t* > **-e-y* > Arm. *-ē*, pl. 2 **e-ykʿ* > *-ē-kʿ* as *berē-kʿ*, follow IE thematic **bhere-ti*, **bhere-te*. Descriptively, the stem finals and endings of II, III, IV are essentially parallel to those of I; various stem types have come to be descriptively identical in all the conjugations, so in I *bere-m* is a simple thematic, while *gorc-e-m* is a (contracted) **-i̯e-* suffix denominative (**13**, 20) from the noun *gorc*, but some characterized stems are obviously such, particularly the numerous ones with nasal formant, cf. the table of principal parts. The present system includes the (mostly prohibitively used with *mi* 'not') present imperative, the neological imperfect indicative, and the neological subjunctive. For all these cf. Select Paradigms, but note also: the ipf. of *em* (*ei*, *ei-r*, *ē-r*; *ea-k'*, *ei-k'*, *ei-n*) has been explained (Lang. 15 [1939], p. 23) as IE opt. **si̯ē-m* recast as pre-Arm. **esī-m* recategorized (for function cf. Welsh and WToch.); phonologically an IE quasi-suffixal aorist stem **esē-*, **esā-* (the latter only in pl. 1 *eak'*, though Lat. ipf. *eram* has it throughout) is equally possible; at all events the imperfects of the regular conjugations are analogous to this, as sg. 1 I, II *bere-i*, III *kay-i*, IV *zenu-i*, cf. paradigms; the prs. subj. of *em* (*içem*, *içes*, *içē*, etc.) implies earlier **isk-* (**ēsk-*?) often compared with OLat. *escit*, etc., with the inflections of a I present indicative; whatever its earlier forms may have been, eventually the first part of the form, *iç-*, came to be the sole marker of its subjunctive function, and the inflections followed the nearest available model; the regular conjugations are again analogous to this, but to some extent with a stronger slanting toward their respectively concurrent presents, as I *beriçem*, III *kayçem*, but II *beriçim*, IV *zenuçum* etc., cf. paradigms.

Aorist stems are of two chief classes: 1. 'strong' (without formant *-ç-*); and 2. 'weak' (with formant *-ç-* < **-sk-*), as sg. 1 (act.) *beri*, *sireçi*, respectively. Broadly speaking, heavily characterized presents are likely to have strong aorists, simple or apparently simple presents weak aorists, but there are many exceptions. Note that while the term 'strong' is descriptively convenient for aorists without formant *-ç*, and a few whole paradigms as sg. 1 *edi*, *etu* seem recast from IE athem. root aorists **e-dhē-m*, **e-dō-m*, as well as for such paradigmatically isolated sg. 3 forms as *e-ber*, *e-lik'* (< ipf. **e-bhere-t*, aor. **e-liqᵘe-t*, indeed uncharacterized) all their other forms imply IE quasi-suffixal *ē-* and *ā-* aorists (> Arm. stem-final *i-* and *a-*), the first occurring in actives (except in pl. 1), *a-* in passives, as pl. 3 act. *beri-n*, pass. *bera-n* (voice distinctions again implemented by different stem finals, but others than those figuring in present stems). This Arm. apportionment of *i-* and *a-* stems (clean cut except in the act. sg. 3, which is endingless, and the pl. 1 act. [stem-final *a-* used in both voices, as *-ak'* act. and pass., cf. ipf. pl. 1 *ea-k'* : *ei-* in most other persons]) is perhaps paralleled in Lith. prts., where stem-final *ė-* < IE *ē-* is more common in transitives, but *o-* < IE *ā-* in intransitives, though it contrasts with Greek, where aorists with suffixal stem-final -η- are specifically intransitive or passive. Note also that a monosyllabic (or augmented, cf. below) sg. 3 act. of a strong aorist often preserves a stem-internal vowel syncopated out of existence in other forms, as *e-lik'* cited above : prs. sg. 1 *lk'ane-m*, aor. sg. 1 *lk'-i*; for the stem-internal *-i-* in this particular verb, cf. Gk. prs. sg. 1 -λιμπάνω (**13**, 10, 11) : aor. ἔλιπον. Note the survival of augment in forms that would otherwise be monosyllabic, as *edi*, *etu*, *eber*, *elik'* above. This is not quite universal even where it would be expected by the rule just given; on the other hand, augment is analogically carried over to a few aor. subj. and ipv. forms! The 'weak' (*-ç-* < **-sk-*) aorists to a considerable extent seem to have been extended from earlier *-ā-* or more commonly *-is-ā-* aorists (cf. Lat. plpf. indic. **-isā-m* > *-era-m*, etc.), as sg. 3 *as-a-ç*, *gorce-a-ç* to *gorce-m*. Weak aorists have the same active and passive inflections as do strong aorists, as sg. 1 act. *gorceç-i*, pass. *gorceç-ay*. The aorist system also includes an ipv. sg. 2 and pl. 2 (affirmatively used), and a subjunctive similarly formed for both strong and weak aorists, active and passive (again with formant *-ç-*, which we earlier, not without some justification, called a morphological maid-of-all-work for Armenian). There are a good many stem-system suppletives, and a few verbs with individual irregularities in stem formation or inflection; some instances of both will be found in the tables of typical principal parts and select paradigms below.

Typical Principal Parts

Ia	Strong aorists			
	prs. sg. 1	aor. sg. 1	(aor. sg. 3)	
1	em	———		
2	berem	beri	eber	
3	acem	aci		
4	bekanem	beki	ebek	
5	gtanem	gti	egit	
6	dizanem	dizi	edēz	
7	dnem	edi	ed	
8	t‘k‘anem	t‘k‘i	et‘uk‘	
9	lk‘anem	lk‘i	elik‘	
10	oṙoganem	oṙogi		
Ib	Weak aorists			
11	gorcem	gorcec̣i		
12	sirem	sirec̣i		
13	gnem	gnec̣i		
14	gitem	gitac̣i		
15	p‘rp‘rem	p‘rp‘rec̣i		
16	ačem	ačec̣i		
17	čašakem	čašakec̣i		
18	amač̣em	amač̣ec̣i		
19	vatnem	vatnec̣i		
20	erdmnec̣uc̣anem	erdmnec̣uc̣uc̣i		(causative)
IIa	Strong aorists			
21	hecanim	hecay		
22	usanim	usay		
23	snanim	snay	snaw (lack of augment due to initial consonant cluster)	
24	ełanim	ełē	(< *ełey)	
25	unim	kalay	(suppl.)	
26	p‘lanim	p‘lay	p‘law (see **23**)	
27	t‘ak‘č̣im	t‘ak‘eay		
28	korač̣im	koreay		
IIb	Weak aorists			
29	dipim	dipec̣ay		
30	erazim	erazec̣ay		
31	gartim	gartec̣ay		
32	bazmim	bazmec̣ay		
33	aysaharim	aysaharec̣ay		

	prs. sg. 1	aor. sg. 1	(aor. sg. 3)	
IIIa	Strong aorists			
34	gam	eki	ekn	
35	tam	etu	et	
36	ert'am	čogay		(suppl.)
IIIb	Weak aorists			
37	gnam	gnaçi	gnaç	(see **23**, **26**)
38	kam	kaçi	ekaç	
39	ałam	ałaçi		
40	lam	laçi	elaç	
41	gt'am	gt'açay		
42	ałbam	ałbaç-i/-ay		
43	ogam	ogaç-i/-ay		
44	orsam	orsaç-i/-ay		
IVa	Strong aorists			
45	gelum	geli	egel	
46	zenum	zeni	ezen	
47	t'ołum	t'ołi	et'oł	
48	lesum	lesi	eles	
49	ǰeṙnum	ǰeṙay		
50	uṙnum	uṙeay		
51	erdnum	erduay (!)		
IVb	Weak aorists			
52	ənkenum	ənkeçi		
53	lnum	lçi	eliç	
54	xnum	xçi	exiç	
55	yenum	yeçay		

Select Paradigms

Prs. ind.	sg.	e-m, e-s, ē; pl. e-mk', ē-k', e-n
	I	bere-m, -s, berē; bere-mk', berē-k', bere-n
	II	beri-m, -s, beri; beri-mk', -k', -n
	III	ka-m, -s, -y; -mk', -yk', -n
	IV	zenu-m, -s, zenu; zenu-mk', -k', -n
		(go-m), (go-s), go-y; (go-mk'), (go-yk'), go-n

Prs. ipv. (prohibitive)		sg. 2 e-r	pl. 2 ē-k, = prs. indic.
	I	bere-r	,,
	II	beri-r	,,
	III	ka-r	,,
	IV	zenu-r	,,

Ipf. ind.		e-i, e-ir, ē-r; e-ak‘, e-ik‘, e-in
	I	bere-i, -ir, ber-ēr; bere-ak‘, -ik‘, -in
	II	same as I bere-i
	III	kay-i, ir, -r; -ak‘, -ik‘, -in
	IV	zenu-i, -ir, zen-oyr; zenu-k‘, -ik‘, -in
		sg. 3 goy-r; pl. 3 goy-in

Prs. subj.		içem	endings same as prs. indic.
	I	beriç-em	
	II	beriç-im	
	III	kayç-em	
	IV	zenuç-um	

sg. 3 guçē < *goyçē

Strong aor. act.	ber-i, -er, e-ber; ber-ak‘, -ēk‘/-ik‘, -in	
Strong aor. m.p.	ber-ay, -ar, -aw; -ak‘, -ayk‘, -an	
Weak aor. act.	sire-ç-i, -er, -ç; -ç-ak‘, -ēk‘/-ik‘, -in	
Weak aor. m.p.	sire-ç-ay, -ar, -aw; -ak‘, -ayk‘, -an	
Strong aor. subj. act.	ber-iç, -çes, -çē; -çuk‘, -ǰik‘, -çen	
Strong aor. subj. m.p.	ber-ayç, -çis, -çi; -çuk‘, -ǰik‘, -çin	
Weak aor. subj. act.	sire-çiç, -sçes, -sçē; -sçuk‘, -sǰik‘, -sçen	
Weak aor. subj. m.p.	sire-çayç, -sçis, -sçi; sçuk‘, -sǰik, -sçin	
Strong aor. ipv. act.	sg. 2 ber	pl. 2 ber-ēk‘
Strong aor. ipv. m.p.	sg. 2 ber-ir	pl. 2 ber-ayk‘
Weak aor. ipv. act.	sg. 2 sire-a	pl. 2 sire-çēk‘
Weak aor. ipv. m.p.	sg. 2 sire-aç	pl. 2 sire-çaruk‘

To some extent aor. pl. 2 m.p. allows a total ending *-aruk‘* (or **-earuk‘* > *-eruk‘*) in the ind. and ipv. beside *-ayk‘*.

West Tocharian. Traces of IE ablaut figure in WT verbal morphology, but there is no such regimented pattern of stem internal ablaut variations apportioned out to particular categories with example after example falling into the same slot as appears in the Gmc. strong verb. There are later quantitative distinctions between e.g., final *-ā* and *-ă* whereby a form historically ending in *-ā* is reduced to *-ă* unless protected by an appended enclitic, as *lyāka* 'he saw' : *lyākā-ne* 'he saw him', and a slightly different one between *-ä-* and *-a-*, both accentually governed, but the rules are not absolute; there are numerous exceptions, whether through analogical interference or scribal error. More nearly predictable is an alternation between non-palatalized consonants or clusters and their palatalized allophones; the general series is:

Non-pal.	k	ŋk	tk	sk	t	tt etc.
Pal.	ś	ṃś, ñś, ñc	cc	ṣṣ	c	cc etc.

Presumably the palatal allophone first stood after IE frontal vowels, so that e.g., **aĝe-* and **sḱe-* would become *āśä-*, *ṣṣä-*, whereas **aĝo-* and **sḱo-*, with which the first mentioned frequently alternated in thematic categories, became *ake-*, *-ske-*; note that the old distribution of the allophones persists, though the actual subsequent vowel changes are considerable, as **e* > *ä*, **o* > *e*. Here, too, there are some departures from the theoretically expected distribution of these allophones; of even greater practical importance is the fact that these allophones, rather than the following vowel that had caused them, were often themselves accepted as markers of a particular verbal category. Thus in the ipf. sg. of a causative verb, the pre-stem final consonant or cluster may have two different morphological claims to a palatal allophone; one because of a following altered stem final *-ī-* (originally optative), and another because it is a causative (probably earlier with stem final *-i̯e-*). Since one consonant or cluster can have but one palatal allophone, WT sometimes also replaces the root initial consonant or cluster with its own palatal allophone regardless of the actually following vowel. Even this, however, is not completely regular; a partial allophone, even on these terms, may not occur when expected, or may appear in a form where it is apparently quite uncalled for.

A verb of either dialect (ET, WT) is cited by its 'root', abstracted from the actual forms in imitation of the procedure of the Sanskrit native grammarians, cf. Table of Principal Parts, below. There are three stem systems: present, subjunctive, preterite (the last largely a conflation of IE perfect and aorist types). Stem-system suppletives occur, some involving two roots, others three or even more.

Present stems fall into twelve classes, of which I, V, and VI are athematic, the rest thematic. A purely morphological classification of these is partly cut across by a functional one into 'primaries' and 'causatives', the latter chiefly in classes VIII-XI, though these also contain what seem to be primaries. Class XII has no causatives but is subdivided into (a) primaries and (b) denominatives. For lack of sufficient amount of text, the actual membership of particular present, subjunctive, or preterite in some classes can only be inferred from non-finite system derivatives, and sometimes even this resource fails us. In the following discussion of classes and the Table of Principal Parts forms are cited, wherever possible, in the sg. 3 (act. *-m*, m.p. *-tär* [normalized from free variants *-tär*, *-trä* in the mss.]); act. prt. with total ending *-a*, m.p. *-te*; other endings, if used, are identified. Occasionally certain endings which have lost an earlier final vowel are extended by *-o*, particularly in metrical texts, to replace the lost vowel.

I. Simple athematics, earlier mostly monosyllabic (**13**, 1); in the active the sg. 3 and pl. 3 have analogically acquired the thematic 'total endings' (i.e., stem final + actual ending) *-äṃ*, *-eṃ* respectively. The actual ending *-ṃ* is from IE secondary *-nt*, but has been analogically extended to the sg. 3, where probable earlier secondary **-t* had been lost; under this functional reapportionment *-ṃ* serves only to express 'third personality', regardless of number; the number difference is carried wholly by preceding *-ä-* < IE **-e-* and *-e-* < **-o-*. In the m.p. the stem was extended, perhaps originally in all persons, by anaptyctic *-a-*; if so, this has been lost by later syncope except in pl. 1 *-a-mtär* and pl. 3 *-a-ntär*.

II. Simple thematics (**13**, 8). Here stem final *-ä-* (< IE **-e-*) palatalizes a preceding consonant, as sg. 3 *aśä-ṃ* : pl. 3 *āke-m*.

III. Like simple thematics, but with stem final WT *-e-* (< IE **-o-*?) generalized; stem final consonants are not palatalized.

IV. Apparently like simple thematics, but with stem final WT *-o-* (of doubtful origin) throughout; no palatalization; stem internal *-o-*, *-ai-*, **au-* only.

V. Athematics apparently of type **13**, 2; stem final *-a-* < IE **-ā-* (generalized major phase); hence both sg. 3 and pl. 3 *-aṃ*; no palatalization.

VI. Athematics (**13**, 5) with IE suffixal *-nā-* (major phase generalized); no palatalization.

VII. Thematics with nasal infix (**13**, 10). Root final *-k-* in eight out of nine cases; note absence of palatal allophone in sg. 3 *piŋkä-m*, not **piŋśä-m*. In classes (VIII), IX, X, XI, all of which contain suffix **-sk(e)-* and some of whose verbs are causatives, we may theorize that these were first made by extending **-sk-* with **-i̯e-* (as **-sk-i̯e-*), which should have produced palatal allophones in all persons (i.e., *-ṣṣ-*). But this did not actually occur, the stem finals remaining as before (i.e., sg. 3 *-ṣṣä-m*, but pl. 1 *-ske-ṃ*, etc.,) and that instead, displaced palatalization in the root initial for a while served as causative marker; in the end, however, as this last change had brought in its train certain accentual and quantitative changes in the interior of the word, it was these changes that marked the causatives, as caus. IXb sg. 1 *kalpäskau* : primary IXa *kälpāskau*.

VIII. Thematics with suffix *-s-* (partly < IE **-s-*, partly **-sk-*, types **13**, 12, 13). Both primaries and causatives occur, with some confusion.

IX. Thematics with suffixal **-sk-*, (**13**, 12.)

X. Thematics with suffixal *-nāsk-*, *-näsk-*, (**13**, 11, 12); root final *-m-* + suffix initial *-n-* > *-mm-*.

XI. Thematics with compound suffix *-sask-*, *-säsk-*, (**13**, 13, 12).

XII. Thematics with compound suffix **-sni̯e-*(?) > *-ññ-*, (**13**, 13, 12, 18).

The present system includes also a neological imperfect and several non-finite forms. The neo-imperfect seems to be a recategorized present optative which had developed imperfect indicative function in addition to its older modal one (cf. Skt. ipf. du. 2, 3 med. *ábharethām*, *-tām* and the Welsh imperfect generally, as sg. 2 *carit*, sg. 3 *carai*). This functional ambiguity led to the emergence of an unambiguous neo-optative (built from the subjunctive, cf. immediately below), the older optative becoming an unambiguous neo-imperfect indicative by relegation. Descriptively the WT ex-optative imperfects are of three classes: (1) for roots *nes-* 'be' and *i-* 'go', we have sg. 1 *ṣaim*, *yaim* (ET *ṣam*, *yem*); *ṣaim* is clearly based on a recasting of IE **si̯ēm* and *yaim* may have been slightly altered analogically to rhyme with it; (2) with altered stem final *-ī-*, apparently from IE generalized minor phase optative marker **-ī-* in simple athematics (as Toch. prs. I), though analogically extended to all thematic classes, combined stem final + marker *-o-i-* in thematics (as prs. II, VII-XII); though it is only where *-ī-* is involved that we should expect palatalization of a pre-stem final consonant (as ex-opt. med. sg. 1 *woloś-tär*), it actually occurs commonly with other thematic classes (as ipf. sg. 3 *nāṣṣi* to prs. II pl. 3 *näskeṃ*); (3) with altered stem final *-oy-* from IE **-āi-* in athematics with stem final *-ā-* to prs. V and VI (as ipf. sg. 3 *lakoy* to prs. V *laka-ṃ*). When the marker *-oy-* is followed e.g., by pl. 3 ending *-e(ṃ)*, contraction may take place, as *-oṃ* < *-oyeṃ*.

Subjunctive stems fall into nearly the same structural classes as present stems, though there are none structurally identical with prs. IV, VII, VIII. There are however, two types structurally different from any present classes, i.e., those with stem final *-i* and *-ñ-*, termed subjunctive IV and VII respectively, in order to keep the number of structurally identical classes as nearly as possible the same. While a present of one class may have a concurrent subjunctive of another, as prs. XI *āksaṣṣä-ṃ* : sbj. II *ākṣä-ṃ*, this is not often the case. Occasionally, when a present and its subjunctive are of the same class, they may show a stem internal quantitative ablaut distinction, as prs. X pl. 3 *tase-ṃ* : sbj. *tāse-ṃ* (here perhaps implying an earlier present : aorist distinction), but often the present and subjunctive are completely identical, and can be distinguished only by their function in context. Note that √*nes* 'be' and √*āk* 'lead' have suppletive sbj. V stems, hence sbj. *tāka-ṃ*, opt. *tākoy* and sbj. *waya-ṃ*, opt. m.p. sg. 1 *wāyoy-mar* : prt. *wāya* respectively. The neo-optative is formed from the subjunctive stem in the same way as the neo-imperfect is from the present stem, hence when the present and subjunctive forms are identical, so also are the imperfect and optative forms. The prehistory of these Tocharian subjunctive classes is unclear. The large number of Class V subjunctives seems to imply that subjunctives originating from IE quasi-suffixal *-ā-* (and *-ē-*?) aorist injunctives were common in pre-Tocharian as in Latin and Old Irish.

Preterite stems fall into six classes (with some subdivisions): I, II, VI are considered 'strong', as containing no obvious suffix marker, whereas III, IV, V are 'weak' because they do. Exception may be taken to this 'strong : weak' grouping, because I-V all imply a pre-Toch. stem final *-ā-*, implying an underlying IE quasi-suffixal *-ā-* (or *-ē-*) aorist or aorist injunctive. This is not the sole source of WT preterites, since most of them are conflated with other IE aorist and/or perfect types, or are, in some of their features, neologisms involving extension of suffix from their concurrent presents.

Prt. I. Short (*-ä-*, *-i-*, *-u-*) root vowels or long (*-ā-*, *-ai-*, *-au-*, -[*o-*?]) designated Ia, Ib respectively. Ablaut plays little or no role in both sub-groups. The root final is irregularly palatalized.

Prt. II. Causatives to present stems in *-äsk-*, *-näsk-*, and *-säsk-* when these have a short root vowel. In contrast to ET the stem is unreduplicated in the finite forms. The root initial is palatalized wherever possible, even *p-*, *m-*, *ts-* frequently > *py-*, *my-*, *tsy-*, and even some cases of *k-* do not > *ś-* but *ky-*.

Prt. III. The *-s-* preterite, but only the act. sg. 3 shows the *-s-*. Conflated from the IE perfect and the *-s-* aorist. Two sub-groups: IIIa, primary, IIIb causative.

Prt. IV is obviously neological, having an *-ṣṣ-* marker extended from presents of class IX (less commonly X, XI); it is seldom primary, mostly causative, as sg. 3 m.p. *karpäṣṣa-te* : prs. IXb *kārpas-trä*. Inflectionally as I, II, with pl. 3 total ending *-a-re*.

Prt. V is also neological, having an *-ñ-* or *-ññ-* marker extended from sbj. VII, as *weña* : sbj. **weñä-ṃ* > *weṃ*, or from prs. XII, as m.p. prt. sg. 3 *kwipeñña-te* : prs. XII m.p. pl. 3 *kwipeññe-ntär*.

Prt. VI (only two examples) is wholly different from all other preterite classes both in stem formation and inflection. It is apparently a lengthened grade aorist, thematicized, but not conflated with any other types, as sg. 3 *śeṃ* probably < **gᵘ̯ēme-t*, (cf. Lat. *vēnit*, Goth. prt. pl. 1 *qēm-um*) and sg. 3 *lac* 'went out' : Xa prs. *lnaṣṣä-ṃ*.

The preterite system also includes two derivative categories: (1) A finite 'durative' or 'intensive preterite' with only a few attested examples, mostly sg. 3, apparently formed from the verb root and extended by *-i-* (as in one type of optative) and the usual preterite endings, as sg. 3 *śawiya* : prs. V, sbj. *śuwaṃ*, ipf., opt. *śuwoy*; and (2) The imperative (rarely from the subjunctive stem), generally with prefix *p*- (!) and special endings for the sg. 2 and pl. 2.

The following Table of Principal Parts lists a selection of roots, then the present, subjunctive, and preterite according to their classes, as described above.

Table of Principal Parts

Root and meaning	Present		Subjunctive		Preterite	
pälk- 'illuminate'	I	palkäṃ			Ia	pälka
käln- 'resound'	I	pl. 3 kalneṃ			IIIa	m.p. kälnsāte
nes- 'be'	I	nesäṃ	V	tākaṃ	Ib	tāka
i- 'go'	I	yaṃ	I	= prs.	III	mas(s)a
āk- 'lead'	II	āśäṃ	V	wayaṃ	Ib	wāya
täs- 'put'	II	pl. 3 taseṃ	II	pl. 3 tāseṃ	Ib	m.p. tasāte
tek- 'disturb'	II	ceśäṃ	I	takäṃ	IIIa	teksa
ṣäm- 'sit'	II	ṣamäṃ	V	lāmaṃ	Ia	lyama
klyaus- 'hear'	II	klyauṣäṃ	II	= prs.	Ib	klyauṣa
pär- 'bear'	II	paräṃ			Ib	m.p. kamāte
käly- 'stand'	II	m.p. kaltär	V	stāmaṃ	Ia	śama
mäsk- 'be'	III	m.p. mäsketär			Ia	maska
sruk- 'die'	III	m.p. sruketär	V	sraukaṃ	Ia	sruka
tsälp- 'go across'	III	m.p. tsälpetär	V	m.p. tsälpātär	Ia	pl. 3 tsälpāre
plānt- 'be satisfied'	IV	m.p. plontotär			Ib	plānta
yāt- 'be capable'	IV	m.p. yototär	V	yātaṃ	Ia	m.p. yatāte
läk- 'see'	V	lakaṃ	V	= prs.	Ib	lyāka
śu-, śwās- 'eat'	V	śūwaṃ	V	= prs.	Ia	śuwa
kwā- 'call'	V	m.p. kwātär	V	m.p. kākatär	Ib	kāka
kärs- 'know'	VI	kärs(a)naṃ	V	kārsaṃ	Ia	śarsa
sik- 'set foot'	VI	siknaṃ	V	saikaṃ		
kaut- 'split'	(VI	inferred fr. ipf.)	V	kautaṃ	Ib	kauta
pik- 'point, write'	VII	piŋkäṃ	V	m.p. paiykatär	Ib	paiyka
putk- 'apportion'	VII	puttaŋkeṃ	V	sg. 1 pautkau		
pärs- 'sprinkle'	VII	präntsäṃ			Ia	m.p. pärsate
er- 'call out'	VIIIa	erṣäṃ	I	m.p. pl. 3 eräntär	III	m.p. ersate
näk- 'destroy, lose'	VIIIa	nakṣäṃ	III	nakäṃ	IIIa	nekṣa
yuk- 'overcome'	VIIIa	yukṣäṃ	V	yūkaṃ	Ia	yuka
pälk- 'burn'	VIIIb	pälkṣäṃ			IIIb	sg. 1 pelykwa
luk- 'shine'	VIIIb	lukṣäṃ			IIIb	lyauksa
räk- 'spread out'	VIIIb	sg. 1 raksau	II	rāśäṃ	IIIb	reksa
wik- 'vanish'	VIIIb	pl. 3 wikseṃ	II	wiśäṃ		
ai- 'give'	IXa	aiṣṣäṃ	I	aiṃ	III	wasa
we- 'say'	IXa	weṣṣäṃ	VII	pl. 3 w(e)ñeṃ	V	weña

Root and meaning	Present	Subjunctive	Preterite
yām- 'make'	IXa yamaṣṣäṃ	I yāmaṃ	IV yamaṣṣa
kälp- 'achieve'	IXa kälpāṣṣäṃ	VI kallaṃ	Ia kalpa
winäsk- 'honor'	IXa wināṣṣäṃ		IV pl. 3 wināṣṣare
kärs- 'know'	IXb śarsäṣṣäṃ		II śārsa
mäsk- 'deceive'	IXb maskäṣṣäṃ		II myāska
yāt- 'be able'	IXb yatṣäṃ		IV m.p. yātäṣṣāte
länt- 'go out'	Xa lnaṣṣäṃ	VII laṃ	VI lac (!)
käl- 'bring'	Xa käläṣṣäṃ	V m.p. kalatär	Ia śala
täm- 'be born'	Xa m.p. tänmastär	III m.p. cmetär	III m.p. temtsate
āks-(1) 'announce'	XIa aksaṣṣäṃ	II ākṣäṃ	Ib ākṣa
āks-(2) 'awake'	XIa (inferred)	V āksaṃ	Ib āksa
su-swās- 'rain'	XIb sg. 1 swāsäskau	XI swāsaṃ	Ib swāsa
käsk- 'destroy'	XIIa käskaṃ	V kāskaṃ	Ia m.p. käskāte
mänt- 'injure'	XIIa mäntaṃ	V m.p. māntatär	
sb. kāwo 'desire'	XIIb m.p. pl. 3 kawaññentär		I m.p. kawāte
sb. kwipe 'shame'	XIIb m.p. pl. 3 kwipeññentär		V m.p. kwipeññate

Select Paradigms (Active Only)

Prs. ind. and sbj.

I sg. 1 *palkau, palkät, palkäṃ; pälkem, palkcer, palkeṃ

II ākau, *äśt, äśäṃ; akem, āścer, ākeṃ

Other stem classes generally similar, apart from matters of stem structure and minor phonological adjustments.

Opt. (built on sbj. stem)

1) yamīm, yamīt, yāmi; yamīyem, yamīcer, yamīyeṃ/yāmyeṃ

2) kärsoym, -oyt, -oy; -oyem, -oycer, -oyeṃ/-oṃ

nes- 'to be' (variously suppleted), tākoym, etc. The underlying sbj. sg. 1 (V) tākau is itself built from the suppletive prt. sg. 3 tāka, etc.; an older opt. sg. 1 ṣaim, ṣait, etc. (probably < IE *si̯ēm) has been recategorized as the ipf. of this verb; analogically WT has developed a regular neo-ipf., which, though built on the present stem, takes opt. endings.

Prt.

1) kaut-āwa, -āsta, -a; (isolated du. 2 -ais); pl. 1 -ām, -ās, -āre

Other classes (except 6) generally similar; pl. 3 sometimes -r.

6) latau, lät, lac; ——, pl. 2 latso, lateṃ

(käm-) sg. 3 śem; pl. 1 kmem, pl. 3 kameṃ

Ipv.

(to prt. sg. 3 klyauṣa) sg. 2 päklyauṣ, pl. 2 (pä)klyauṣṣo

Old Church Slavic. Two (or three) stem systems: present, aorist, (infinitive). There is close relationship between many aorist stems and their concurrent infinitive stems, but the two are not always identical. Many verbs have more than one aorist, at least in certain persons, but only one infinitive. At least one type of aorist (apparently growing in numbers in later OCS) is virtually a derivative category of the present stem, as sg. *nesochъ* : prs. *nesǫ*. An over-all classification of OCS verbs can be based either on their present stems or their infinitive stems. Our Table of Principal Parts is essentially a condensation of Stang's present-stem classification, with subdivisions involving infinitive and aorist concurrences.

Present stems are classified as (I) Athematic (sg. 1 *-mь*, sg. 2 mostly *-si*, pl. 3 *-ętъ*), (II) Half-Thematic (sg. 1 *-jǫ*, sg. 2 *-i-ši*, pl. 3 *-ętъ*), (III) Thematic (sg. 1 *-ǫ* or *-jǫ*, sg. 2 *-e-ši* or *-je-ši*, pl. 3 *-ǫtъ*). Class I consists of four old simple stems (**13**, 1) : IE **es-mi* > OCS *jes-mь*, **ēd-mi* > *ja-mь* (but with preverbs *-ě-mь*) and probably **dō-mi* > *da-mь* (though a reduplicated preform **dōd-mi* is often set up for this last to explain its sg. 3 *das-tъ* and pl. 3 *dad-ętъ*, which can as well be regarded as analogical to *jas-tъ*, *jad-ętъ*); **u̯oi̯d-mi* analogically recast from IE pf. m.p. **u̯oi̯d-ai* > OCS *věmь* (with an isolated byform *vědě* < **u̯oi̯d-ai*); the major phase is generalized except in pl. 3 *sǫtъ* 'are.' Class I also includes isolated (**13**, 2) *imamь*, sg. 2 *ima-si*, pl. 3 *im-ǫtъ*. Class II involves the same problems as do the half-thematic presents of Italic, Celtic, Germanic(?), and Baltic; in some instances the stem final *-ī-* (so Slavic, in contrast to Baltic *-i-*) may be a post-IE contraction of **-ei̯e-*, and in others of some other origin. Class III may be subdivided in its own right according to the presence or absence of various formants, and also according to Brugmann's accentual types A and B (e.g., sg. 3 *bere-tъ* is of type A, sg. 3 *mьre-tъ* of type B) or, with still greater complexities, according to the types of concurrent aorist and infinitive stems; our Table of Principal Parts will show some of the actual concurrences. A noteworthy feature of all class III presents is that they show stem final *-e-* rather than expected *-o-* in the du. 1 and pl. 1 (e.g., pl. 1 Gk. φέρο-μεν, Goth. *baira-m*, OCS *bere-mъ*); this seems to have spread from forms with *-i̯e-* suffix, where the shift of *o* > *e* is phonological, as in pl. 1 *znaje-mъ*. Stem final *-o-* (not *-e-*) does occur in the du. 1 and pl. 1 of thematic aorists, as in pl. 1 *sědo-mъ*, not only in aorists inherited as such (where, of course, the formant *-i̯e-* would not occur), but also in one-time imperfects which have become aorists by later relegation, as *reko-mъ* in contrast to prs. *reče-mъ*.

Infinitives always end in *-ti*, as in Lithuanian and West Tocharian (*-tsi*), historically some oblique case of an IE verbal noun. Infinitive stems have long been conventionally classified in six groups: (1) monosyllabic, i.e., without extension, as *nes-ti*, *by-ti*, *sta-ti*, and groups 2-6, with real or apparent stem extension; (2) *-nǫ-*, as *dvignǫ-ti*; (3) *-ě-*, as *umě-ti*; (4) *-i-*, as *nosi-ti*; (5) *-a-*, *děla-ti*; (6) *-ova-* (really a special case of 5), *darova-ti*; for further examples cf. Table of Principal Parts. Slavic dictionaries usually cite the sg. 1, sg. 2, and infinitive of every verb, which can thus be readily classified under either the present-stem or infinitive-stem schemes.

Aorist stems can be classified in three groups, with subdivisions in each group, as (1) non-*s*- aorists; (2) *s*- aorists not drastically recast; and (3) Slavic neologically recast *s*-aorists (so-called *-ochъ* aorists).

(1. 1) Thematic type (sg. 1 IE *-o-m* > OCS *-ъ*), some of these showing different stem

internal vocalism or different stem structure from the present, as sg. 1 *sědъ* : prs. *sędǫ*, *dvigъ* : prs. *dvignǫ*, both probably IE aorists, even if somewhat recast. Others, as *vedъ* : prs. *vedǫ* are old imperfects, relegated to aorist function by the emergence of the Slavic neo-imperfect, see below. Many 1. 1 aorists occur especially or only in the sg. 2, 3 (IE **-e-s, *-e-t* both > OCS *-e*), as *sěde, dvize, vede*, to supplete other aorists not formed in the sg. 2, 3.

(1. 2) Monosyllabic sg. 2 forms in *-ě, -a*, etc. The oldest of these may be survivals from old athematic root aorists, as **(e)dō-s, -t* both > OCS *da*, **(e)stā-s, -t* both > OCS *sta*, but since they occur only in paradigms whose other persons and numbers are clearly *s*-aorists (as sg. 1 *dachъ, stachъ*, cf. below), and since plausible *s*-aorist preforms sg. 2 **-s-s*, sg. 3 **-s-t* would > the same OCS forms, it is not clear whether OCS *da, sta*, etc., are true survivals of non-*s*-aorists or conflations of non-*s* and *s*-types. Whatever their origin, they have given rise to such partly analogical forms as sg. 2, 3 *kry, ču, pi, pę, mrě* (: sg. 1 *krychъ, čuchъ, pichъ, pęchъ, mrěchъ*).

(1. 3) Dissyllabic etc., sg. 2, 3 forms in *-a, -ě* may survive from old quasi-suffixal *-ē-* and *-ā-* aorists, as IE **(e)bherā-s, -t* > OCS *bьra* : OCS prs. sg. 1 *berǫ*; **(e)menē-s, -t* > OCS *mьně* : prs. sg. 1 *mьnjǫ* (but the stem internal vocalism of such IE preforms may have been reduced under ablaut conditions from **-e-* to IE shwa secundum, in which event OCS *bьra* reflects the IE more precisely than Lat. *feras*, OIr. *bera*). The case for the truly suffixal nature of *-a-* is clear enough in the example given, where the present shows no trace of this *-a-*; it is not clear for the *ě*-aorists, as even in the example given, differing reductions of a base **menēi̯-* might figure in both present and aorist. Both, however, have given rise to analogical forms in which the *-a* or *-ě* obviously figures in the present also, as aor. sg. 2, 3 *děla, umě* : prs. sg. 1 *dělajǫ, uměјǫ*. Exactly the same uncertainty occurs here as with *da, sta* above; we do not know whether *bьra* etc., are unquestionable survivals of a non-*s*-aorist or possible conflations with an *s*-aorist (sg. 1 *bьrachъ, mьněchъ* etc.). Whatever their origin, they have served as models for such analogical forms as sg. 2, 3 *rinǫ, moli, darova* (sg. 1 *rinǫchъ, molichъ, darovachъ*, etc.). It is interesting to compare the fortunes of the IE quasi-suffixal *-ā-, -ē-* aorists in Baltic, where (even if only in virtue of wide analogical spread and some recasting of both presents and preterites) their *-ā-, -ē-* came to be obviously suffixal, dominating the entire Baltic preterite, without any competition from *s*-aorists, whereas in Slavic any unrecast survival of them as suffixal is doubtful, and they have been mostly swallowed up in *s*-aorist recastings (cf. below), even though these recastings in sg. 1 *-āchъ, -ěchъ* have served as models for such neologisms as sg. 1 *-ǫchъ, -ichъ, -ovachъ*, etc.

(2. 1) IE *s*-aorists, basically an *-s-* reinforcement of the old lengthened grade athematic root aorist, as **u̯ēĝh-* (cf. Goth. prt. pl. *wēg-*) to **u̯ēk̑-s-* (cf. Skt. aor. sg. 1 *á-vākṣ-am*, Lat. 'pf.' *vēx-ī*) > OCS *věsъ*, to prs. *vezǫ*, or **bhōdh-* (cf. Lat. pf. *fōd-ī*) to **bhōt-s-* > OCS *basъ* to prs. *bodǫ*; eventually probably formed *de novo* from other aorists and indeed presents. Though historically athematic, this type was thematicized in PSlavic in the sg. 1, du. 1, pl. 1, giving total endings sg. 1 **-so-m*, etc., whence OCS sg. 1 *-sъ*, du. 1 *-so-vě*, pl. 1 *-so-mъ*, as against (e.g.) pl. 2 **-s-te*, pl. 3 **-s-n̥t* > OCS *-sę*.

(2. 2) This is really only an allophone variant of 2. 1. PSlav. *-s-*, when standing between *i, u, r, k* and any vowel, > *-ch-*; thus sg. 1 **būso-m* > *bychъ*, and similarly du. 1 *bychově*,

pl. 1 *bychomъ*; in the pl. 3 **bychę* underwent secondary palatalization to *byšę*. Analogically these total endings *-chъ, -chově, -chomъ, -šę* came to be used after any vowel, including those due to Slavic liquid + consonant metathesis, so that e.g., PSlav. sg. 1 **kolsom, *mersom* > OCS *klachъ, mrěchъ* (sg. 2, 3 *kla, mrě*); actually the 2. 2 aorists came to outnumber those of 2. 1, though in a few instances both occur (sg. 1 *pęsъ/pęchъ*).

(3) Neologically recast *s*-aorists. In early OCS times (?) such coexisting forms as pl. 1 (1. 1) *rekomъ*, (2. 2) *rěchomъ* produced a conflation *rekochomъ*, eventually expanded to a whole new type built from the present stem, sg. 1 *rekochъ*, etc., whence its name '*-ochъ*-aorist', but otherwise following 2. 2. Though rare or non-existent in the earliest texts, this came to be the most common type in the later texts. Except for the doubtful cases discussed under 1. 2 and 1. 3, no Slav. *s*-aorists form a sg. 2, 3; these forms are regularly supplied by non-*s* types.

The infinitive and aorist stem also includes the neo-imperfect in sg. 1 *-ěachъ/-aachъ*, which is tentatively explained as a coalesced periphrastic whose second member is an appended auxiliary sg. 1 **ēsom* etc., i.e., a thematicized lengthened grade aorist, or less probably an augmented (!) imperfect of **es* 'be', with analogical *-ch-* for expected *-s-* after numerous 2. 2 aorists. The first member of the periphrasis might have been a verbal noun in some oblique case (cf. Lat. neo-ipf. *vehēbam*, etc.); this member usually ends in *-ě-* (*nesěachъ*), but in *-a-* when the infinitive is in *-ati* (*děla-achъ*), and under certain other phonological conditions, cf. Select Paradigms, below. In the latest OCS texts the neo-imperfect of verbs in sg. 1 *-ujǫ*, inf. *-ovati* is sometimes formed from the present stem, as sg. 1 *daruja- achъ* beside normal *darovachъ*. For the survival or loss of the aorists and the neo-imperfect in modern Slavic languages see the end of this appendix.

Typical Principal Parts

	§ **13**	Present	Infinitive	Aor. 1.1, 1.2	Aor. 1.3	Aor. 2.1, 2.2	Aor. 3
I	1	jesmь	1 byti	sg. 2, 3 bě		bychъ	
	1	jamь	1 jasti	sg. 2, 3 -ě		jasъ	
	1	damь	1 dati	sg. 2, 3 da		dachъ	
	1	věmь	3 věděti		sg. 2, 3 vědě	věděchъ	
	2	imamь	3 iměti		sg. 2, 3 imě	iměchъ	
II	25	nošǫ, -siši	4 nositi		sg. 2, 3 nosi	nosichъ	
		mьnjǫ, -iši	3 mьněti		sg. 2, 3 mьně	mьněchъ	
		slyšo, -iši	5 slyšati		sg. 2, 3 slyša	slyšachъ	
III	8A	nesǫ, -eši	1 nesti	sg. 2, 3 nese		něsъ	nesochъ
		bodǫ	1 bosti	sg. 2, 3 bode		basъ	bodochъ
		rekǫ	1 rešti	sg. 2, 3 reče		rěchъ	rekochъ
		berǫ	5 bьrati		sg. 2, 3 bьra	bьrachъ	
	8B	mьrǫ	1 mrěti	sg. 2, 3 mrě		mrěchъ	
	9, 18	deždǫ	1 děti	sg. 2, 3 dě			
	10	sędǫ	1 sěsti	sědъ			
	10, 18	-ręštǫ	1 -ręsti	-rětъ			-rětochъ

§ 13	Present	Infinitive	Aor. 1.1, 1.2	Aor. 1.3	Aor. 2.1, 2.2	Aor. 3
11	stanǫ	1 stati	sg. 2, 3 sta		stachъ	
	dvignǫ	2 dvignǫti	dvigъ			dvigochъ
	rinǫ	2 rinǫti	sg. 2, 3 rinǫ		rinǫchъ	
18	znajǫ	1 znati	sg. 2, 3 zna		znachъ	
19	dělajǫ	5 dělati		sg. 2, 3 děla	dělachъ	
20	uměјǫ	3 uměti		sg. 2, 3 umě	uměchъ	
23	darujǫ	6 darovati		sg. 2, 3 darova	darovachъ	
15 16	idǫ	1 iti	id			idochъ
17	živǫ	1 žiti	sg. 2, 3 ži		žichъ	

Select Paradigms

Prs.	I	jes-mь, -si, -tъ; -vě, -ta, -te; -mъ, -te, sǫtъ
		ja-mь, -si, -stъ; -vě, -sta, -ste; -mъ, -ste, -dętъ
		da-mь, -si, -stъ; -vě, -sta, -ste; -mъ, -ste, -dętъ
		vě-mь, -si, -stъ; -vě, -sta, -ste; -mъ, -ste, -dętъ
		ima-mь, -ti, -tъ; -vě, -ta, -te; -mъ, -te, imǫtъ
	II	mьn-jǫ, -iši, -itъ; -vě, -ita, -ite; -imъ, -ite, -ętъ
	III	nes-ǫ, -eši, -etъ; -evě, -eta, -ete; -emъ, -ete, -ǫtъ
Ipv.	I	sg. 2, 3 jaždь; du. 1 jadi-vě, du. 2 -ta; pl. 1 -mъ, pl. 2 -te
		(The ipv. of the vb. 'to be' is suppletive and thematic, and inflected in all persons and numbers: bǫd-emь, -i, -i; -ěvě, -ěta, -ěte; -ěmъ, -ěte, -ǫ)
	II	sg. 2, 3 mьn-i; du. 1 -i-vě, du. 2 -ta; pl. 1 -mъ, pl. 2 -te
	III	ber-i; -ěvě, -ěta; -ěmъ, -ěte
		znaji; -vě, -ta; -mъ, -te
Aor.	1.1	sěd-ъ, sg. 2, 3 -e; -ově, -eta, -ete; -omъ, -ete, -ǫ
		dvi-gъ, sg. 2, 3 -že; -gově, -žeta, -žete; -gomъ, -žete, -gǫ
		(In many verbs a 1.1 aorist occurs only in the sg. 2, 3.)
	1.2	occurs only in the sg. 2, 3, as by, da, sta, pi, etc. Some verbs also allow extended forms, as bystъ, dastъ, pitъ, variously explained.
	1.3	also occurs only in the sg. 2, 3, as bâra, umě, etc.
	2.1	bas-ъ, (no sg. 2, 3); -ově, -ta, -te; -omъ, -te, -ę
	2.2	rěchъ; rěchově, rěs-ta, -te; rěchomъ, rěste, rěšę
	3	reko-chъ; -chově, -sta, -ste; -chomъ, -ste, -šę
Ipf.		nesě-achъ, sg. 2, 3 -aše; -achově, -ašeta, -ašete; -achomъ, -atete, -achǫ
		bьra-achъ, etc. (first member ends everywhere in *-a*).

The verb system and inflections of the other Slavic languages must have been fairly similar to those of OCS during the period of our OCS texts. Even then there was emerging a functional distinction between verbs of 'perfective aspect' (implying completion of action, etc.) and those of 'imperfective aspect' (implying non-completion of action). This functional distinction, though not as yet fully worked out in OCS, came in time to dominate the entire Slavic verb system, so much so that we now expect to find for every verb concept two distinct verbs, one 'pfv.' anther 'impfv.', and sometimes still others for various minor aspects. Sometimes, indeed, the two chief aspects are etymologically unrelated, as OCS *rešti* 'to say' (pfv.) : *glagolati* 'to speak' (impfv.); sometimes the two involve different stem formation from the same lexeme, as **padti* > *pasti* (pfv.) : *padati* (impfv.), or finally, the addition of a preverb (sometimes coloring the meaning in non-aspectual ways also) to form a pfv. from an impv. On the whole the aspectual system in its eventual rigidity is best regarded as a specifically Slavic innovation, though some of the conceptual potentialities for its ultimate growth may have been inherited from IE.

An important morphological development has been the use of a one-time periphrastic perfect (formed from the infinitive stem with endings sg. masc. *-lъ*, fem. *-la*, neut. *-lo*, du. masc. *-la*, fem., neut. *-lě*, pl. masc. *-li*, fem. *-ly*, neut. *-la*, agreeing with the subject, and using the verb 'to be' as its auxiliary) to replace both the OCS aorist and imperfect. Instances of this occur even in OCS texts; thus, the NT passage (John 17. 22) . . . ἣν δέδωκάς (pf. sg. 2) μοι δέδωκα (pf. sg. 1) αὐτοῖς '. . . which Thou hast given me I have given them' is translated *jęže dalъ jesi* (periphrastic sg. 2 masc.) *mně, dachъ* (aor. sg. 1) *jimъ*. In this case the ambiguity of aor. *da*, which might be either sg. 2 or sg. 3, may have turned the scales in favor of the unambiguous periphrastic, but with the increasing domination of aspect, there was less and less need for a perfect as such, and the periphrastic of verbs now clearly perfective tended more and more to replace their aorists, and that of verbs now clearly imperfective tended to replace their imperfects, while the auxiliary came to be freely dropped (as always in New Russian). Meanwhile the old aorist and imperfect became obsolete in most Slavic languages by about 1500, though they survive languidly even today in Bulgarian, Serbo-Croatian, and Wendish. Non-prestige dialects of Eastern Czech and Slovak show interesting conflations of the periphrastics with the tag *-ch-* of the older tenses, as sg. 1, 3 masc. *nesl-ch*, fem. *nesla-ch*, and even such drastic dislocation of morphemes as *oba-ch-me plakali* 'we both wept' (quoted by Vondrák, *Vgl. Slav. Gram.* ii 198 from the Czech specialist J. Gebauer).

Lithuanian. Three tense systems: present, preterite (based on IE aorists), infinitive (also largely based on IE aorists, and including a number of finite categories). Seven classes of present stems have been recognized: I. Simple thematics (**13**, 8), but also others with formant *-in-* or *-en-* (**13**, 11 and a variant) extended to the whole paradigm; II. Thematics with nasal infix (**13**, 10), including some verbs with pre-stem final *-l* and *-r*, in strong contrast to the limitation on nasal-infix presents in Old Irish and their almost complete absence in OCS (four examples) and Gothic (one example, *standen*). This class also includes a few with suffixal *-ne* (**13**, 11, not extended); III. Thematics with dental suffix (mostly as Lith. *-ste*, somehow related to **13**, 14). I-III are identically inflected, as sg. 1 *-u*, sg. 2 *-i*, sg. 3 *-a*, pl. 1 *-a-me*, etc.; IV. Thematics with suffix **-i̯e* (**13**, 18), including many denominatives, inflected as sg. 1 *-iu* (postvocalic *-ju*), sg. 2 *-i* or *-ji*, sg. 3 *-ia* or *-ja*, pl. 1 *-iame* or *-jame*; V. Half thematics inflected sg. 1 *-iu*, sg. 2, 3 *-i*, pl. 1 *-ime*, etc.; VI. Athematics with quasi-suffixal *-ā* (**13**, 2), with sg. 1 *-au* (analogically recast for expected **-ō-mi*), sg. 2 *-ai*, sg. 3 *-o*, pl. 1 *-o-me*, etc.: VII. Old monosyllabic athematics with sg. 1 *-mi* (recast in NLith. as thematics of various classes). If we group these in 'conjugations' according to present inflections (as in Latin and Armenian), classes I, II, III form a single conjugation, each of the others a separate one.

Some preterite stems began as IE zero-grade thematic aorists, others as lengthened-grade athematic aorists, Lith. stem-internal *-ė-*, *-o-* : prs. *-e-*, *-a-*, though those with *-y-*, *-ū-* : prs. *-i-*, *-u-* are analogical (otherwise Stang, Vgl. Balt. Gram., p. 389); still others of the quasi-suffixal IE **-ē-*, **-ā-* type. Eventually all aorists not of this last type were recast as such, sometimes retaining an older distinctive stem-internal vocalism. But as this **-ē-*, **-ā-* came to be the chief distinguishing mark of all preterites, many newer preterites were formed, or older ones recast, simply by the addition of the suffix, while agreeing with their concurrent presents in stem-internal vocalism. If we regard only the ultimate stem-final vocalism, there are basically only two classes of preterites: (1) Those in sg. 1 **-ē-ō*, sg. 3 **ē-t* > Lith. *-iau*, *-ė*, and (2) sg. 1 **-ā-ō*, sg. 3 **-ā-t* > Lith. *-au*, *-o*, etc. Note the use of sg. 1 *-ō* ending in preterital forms, as to some extent in Celtic, etc., also. This apparently simple classification, however, is complicated in two different ways: first, the infinitive stem also was perhaps sometimes built from these suffixal aorist stems, or at least later analogically extended in the same way by Lith. *-ė* or *-ō*; when this happens the preterite stem receives an additional **-ā* extension, whereby older sg. 1 *-iau*, *-au* then > respectively *-ėjau*, *-ōjau* (*-j-* apparently a glide or hiatus breaker); such preterites are listed here as 1x or 2x respectively. We show identity or difference of stem-internal vocalism among the three stems by adding: 1 when all three agree in this respect; 2 when the present and preterite agree as against the infinitive; 3 when the present and infinitive agree as against the preterite; 4 when the preterite and infinitive agree as against the present; and 5 when all three are distinct.

Infinitives (except when followed by the enclitic reflexive *-s*) end in *-ti*, as in OCS and WToch. (*-tsi*). They can be classified as 1 when they show no stem extension, as 2 when actually or apparently extended by *-ė*, as 3 when by *-ō*, and as 4 when by *-y* (this last, despite its half-thematic appearance, occurring only concurrently with certain presents of class VI having preterites of class 2). Relations in stem-internal vocalism are shown in the same manner as in preterite stems. The infinitive stem also occurs in the future, (where it is followed by *-s-* marker and present class V inflections, as sg. 1 *dirbsiu*, sg. 2 *dirbsi*, etc.,) in the neo-imperfect (followed by sg. 1 *-davau*, like a class 2 preterite, as *dìrbdavau*), and in the neo-imperative (followed by sg. 2 *-k*, pl. 1 *-ki-me*, etc., like class V presents). The so-called optative (a semicoalesced periphrasis) has as its first member a 'supine' (= infinitive, but with historical ending *-tum*, so still, except sg. 3 *-tų*, where the auxiliary is dropped). In the sg. 1 the supine has been completely 'telescoped' with the auxiliary (itself an old optative, now no longer used independently), i.e., *-tų* + *-biau* > *-čiau*; cf. paradigms. Differences of pattern in accent placement and intonational quality among the three systems will not be discussed here.

Typical Principal Parts

		prs. sg. 1		prt. sg. 1		infinitive
1	I	liekù	2.4	likaũ	1	lìkti
2		perkù	2.4	pirkaũ	1	pir̃kti

		prs. sg. 1		prt. sg. 1		infinitive
3		dìrbu	2.1	dìrbau	1	dìrbti
4		vežù	1.1	vežiaũ	1	vèžti
5		menù	1.4	miniaũ	1	miñti
6		tekù	1×.1	tekė́jau	2	tekė́ti
7		bìldu	1×.1	bildė́jau	2	bildė́ti
8		miegù	2×.1	miegójau	3	miegóti
9		imù	1.3	ėmiaũ	1	im̃ti
10		malù	1.1	maliaũ	1	málti
11		pinù	1.3	pýniau	1	pìnti
12		puolù	1.2	púoliau	1	pùlti
13		alsinù	2.1	alsinaũ	1	alsìnti
14		gyvenù	2.1	gyvenaũ	1	gyvénti
15	II	randù	2.1	radaũ	1	ràsti
16		tampù	1.1	tapiaũ	1	tàpti
17		bąlù	2.1	balaũ	1	bálti
18		gáunu	2.1	gavaũ	1	gáuti
19	III	saustù	2.1	sausaũ	1	saũsti
20		mė́gstu	2.1	mė́gau	1	mė́gti
21		mìrštu	1.1	miriaũ	1	mir̃ti
22		vérdu	1.4	viriaũ	1	vìrti
23	IV	keliù	1.3	kė́liau	1	kélti
24		slepiù	1.3	slėpiaũ	1	slė̃pti
25		skiriù	1.3	skýriau	1	skìrti
26		kariù	1.3	kóriau	1	kárti
27	IV	vagiù	1.3	vogiaũ	1	vógti
28		sė́ju	2.1	sė́jau	1	sė́ti
29		plóju	2.1	plójau	1	plóti
30		gyjù	2.4	gijaũ	1	gýti
31		šlúoju	1.4	šlaviaũ	1	šlúoti
32		pláuju	1.4	plóviau	1	pláuti
33		dovanóju	2×	dovanójau	3	dovanóti
34		áuklėju	2×	áuklėjau	2	áuklėti
35		dalyjù	2×	dalyjaũ	4	dalýti
36		klastúoju	2×	klastavaũ	5	klastúoti
37		keliáuju	2×	keliavaũ	6	keliáuti
38	V	mýliu	2×	mylė́jau	2	mylė́ti
39	VI	žinaũ	2×	žinójau	3	žinóti
40		sakaũ	1	sakiaũ	4	sakýti

		prs. sg. 1		prt. sg. 1		infinitive
41	VII	esmì 'am'	2	! buvaũ	1	búti
42		eimì 'go'	2	ėjaũ	1	eĩti
43		ė̃(d)mi 'eat'	1.1	ė̃džiau	1	ė̃sti
44		dúomi 'give'	1	daviaũ	1	dúoti
45		dė̃mi 'put'	1.1	dė̃jau	1	dė̃ti

NLith. substitutes: for 41 esmì; esù, yrà, ẽsame
for 42 eimì; einù, etc.
for 44 dúomi; dúodu, etc.
for 45 dė̃mi; dedù, etc.

Select Paradigms

(In all Lith. mood-tense categories the sg. 3 suppletes the missing du. 3 and pl. 3)

Prs.	I, II, III	sg. dìrb-u, -i, -a; du. -ava, -ata; pl. -ame, -ate
	IV	plój-u, -i, -a; -ava, -ata; -ame, -ate
	IV	keli-ù, -ì, -a; -ava, -ata; -ame, -ate
	V	mýli-u, mýli, mýl(i); mýli-va, -ta; -me, -te
	VI	sak-aũ, -aĩ, -o; -ova, -ota; -ome, -ote
	VII (OLith)	es-mì, -ì, -t(i); -và, -tà; -mè, -tè
		ė̃(d)mi, ? , ė̃s-t(i); ? , ? ; ? , ?
		ei-mì, -sì, -t(i); -và, -tà; -mè, -te
		dúo-mi, -si, -t(i); -va, -ta; -me, -ste
		dė̃-mi, -si, -ti; ? , ? ; -me, -ste

(The stem-final -*s* in sg. 3 (and pl. 2?) of ė̃(d)mi is a cluster development < *-*d*-*t*; that in the same forms of dúomi, dė̃mi is analogical to this.)

Prt.	1	kė̃l-iau, -eĩ, -ė; -ėva, -ėta; -ė̃me, -ėte
	2	dìrb-au, -ai, -o; -ova, -ota; -ome, -ote

(So, too, apart from accentual and intonational differences, all other preterites)

Ipf.	dìrb-davau, -davai, -davo; -davova, -davota; -davome, -davote
	(So, e.g., pló-davau, kél-davau, mylė̃-davau)
Fut.	dìrbs-iu, -si, -s; -iva, -ita; -ime, -ite
	(So, e.g., plós-iu, mylė̃s-iu, sakýs-iu, etc.)
Ipv.	sg. 2 dìrbk; du. 1 -iva, du. 2 -ita; pl. 1 -ime, pl. 2 -ite
	(So, e.g., plók, kélk, mylė̃k, sakýk, etc.)

The so-called optative has the semi-coalesced auxiliary element: sg. 1 -čiau, -bei, -(zero); -biva, -bita; -bime, -bite, hence,

dìrb-čiau, -tum-bei, -tų; -tum-biva, -bita; -bime, -bite

Albanian. It is very difficult to equate the Albanian situation with IE. Texts are late, and massive contacts with (non-IE) Turkish and Arab speakers as well as those of other IE languages have both overloaded the vocabulary and severely distorted the probable earlier typology of the language. Strong stress accent, perhaps at various periods, has effected drastic syncope, cf. _ftet_ < Lat. _veritatem_ and _-fsha_ < Lat. _-vissem_. All forms cited are Standard or Central Albanian, as far as we can tell.

The verb has two tense systems, present and aorist. We number the presents arbitrarily as follows: I, apparently simple athematics (type **13**, 1), with just three verbs, _jam_ 'am' (< _*es-mi_), _kam_ 'have' (< _*qap-mi_ or _*qab(h)-mi_), _them_ 'say' (< _*k̂n̥s-mi_); II, apparently simple thematics with neo-final unpalatalized consonants, as _prish_ 'destroy', occasionally, perhaps, with vestigial formants or quasi-formants, as _*marn-_ > Alb. _marr_ (aor. _mora_) 'take'; III, thematics with neo-final vowel, not nasalized, as _rri_ 'sit.' Some of these have unquestionably lost a final consonant, as sg. 1, 2, 3 _bi_ 'bring', while others probably are **13**, 18 IE formations; IV, thematics with sg. 1 _-s_, sg. 3 _-t_, as _rris, rrit_ 'raise', _fus, fut_ 'put in.' The sg. 1 _-s_ < _*-t-i̯ō_, in which the _-t_ may be a root final or quasi-formant. Many such verbs are said to be loans based on Slavic infinitives in _-i-ti_ (Meyer § 93). In any event, the prs. sg. 2, 3 were pre-Alb. _*-i̯e-s_, _*-i̯e-t_ or half-thematic _*is_, _*-it_, either capable of umlauting non-frontal stem internal vowels, hence sg. 1 _flas_, sg. 2, 3 _flet_ 'speak', etc. For the neo-personal ending _-ni_ (cf. immediately below), hence pl. 1 _flas-im_, pl. 3 _flas-in_, but pl. 2 _flit-ni_; V, thematics with sg. 1 _-j_, sg. 3 _-n_, as _punòj_, _punòn_ 'work', _vê_ 'put'. The sg. 1 _-j_ <_*-n-i̯ō_; sg. 2, 3 < _*-n̥i̯es/-nis_, _*-n̥i̯e-/*-ni-t_. The _-n-_ in some cases may imply IE **13**, 11, 18, in others it may be a stem final. It is from this class that the neo-ending pl. 2 _-ni_ < _*-n-īe-te_ or _*-n-i-te_ has developed. It spread to all presents (and imperatives), often but not always umlauting a stem-internal vowel (the absence of this effect in some contemporary forms may be analogical and relatively recent), thus to sg. 1 _jam_, Meyer has pl. 2 _jini_, Pekemezi _jini_ or 'Gheg _jeni_', Hasluck only _jeni_. The neo-ending _-ni_ has not displaced _-te/-t_ in the imperfect, aorist, and optative. The present system includes the present indicative, imperfect indicative, present subjunctive (with introductory particle _të_), imperative, and is also an element in certain periphrastics.

The aorists we number arbitrarily as: Ia, strong aorist with stem internal lengthened grade ablaut (+ IE _-ē_> Alb. _-o_), as prs. sg. 1, 3, _pjek_, aor. sg. 1 _poqa_, prs. sg. 1 _flas_, sg. 3 _flet_, aor. sg. 1 _fola_; Ib, strong aorist, with same internal stem vowel as the present stem, as prs. sg. 1 _vesh_, aor. sg. 1 _vesha_ 'clothe, dress', prs. sg. 1 _prish_, aor. sg. 1 _prisha_ 'destroy'; Ic, strong aorist, perhaps occasionally with distinct stem internal vowel not due to IE ablaut. Suppletive aorists are fairly common in this and other classes, as prs. _bi_ 'bring', aor. _prûna_; 2, _-s-_ aorists, presumably from IE, although observable only in the sg. 1, as _thashë_ to prs. _them_ 'say', _desha_ to prs. _du_ 'wish, love', and inflection of other persons as in aorist 1; 3, _-(o)va_ (the _-va_ conjectured to be a loan from Lat. ipf.! sg. 1 _-bam_, etc.), weak aorist, as _punova_ to prs. _punòj_ 'work', aor. _dava_ to prs. _daj, dan_ 'separate.' The aorist system includes the aorist indicative and the coalesced periphrastic optative (_-fsha_ conjectured < Latin perfect subjunctive _-vissem_ [so Meyer, Alb. Gr. § 110]).

The 'Table of Principal Parts' will list the prs. sg. 1 and sg. 3, and aor. sg. 1. Present classes will have Roman numerals, aorist classes Arabic numerals.

Table of Principal Parts

Prs.	sg. 1	meaning	sg. 3	aor.	sg. 1
I	jam	be	âsht	2	qeshë
	kam	have	ka	1b	pata
	them	say	thotë	2	thashë
II	prish	destroy	prish	1b	prisha
	dal	come out	del	1a	dola
	(j)ap	(j)ep	(j)ep		dhashë
	shof	see	shef	2	pashë
	fal	pardon	fal	1b	fala
	marr	take	merr	1a	mora
	vesh	clothe	vesh	1b	vesha
III	bi	bring	bi	1c	prûna
	bi	fall	bi	2	rashë
	du	love	do	2	desha
	rri	sit	rri	1c	ndêj(t)a
	pi	drink	pi	3	piva
	di	know	di	1b	dita
IV	rris	raise	rrit	1b	rrita
	bërtàs	call out	bërtèt	1b	bertita
	fus	put in	fut	1b	futa
	grabis	steal	grabit	1b	grabita
	pres	expect	pret	1b	prita
	shes	sell	shet	1b	shita
	flas	speak	flet	1a	fola
V	punòj	work	punòn	3	punova
	dërgòj	send	dërgòn	3	dergova
	banòj	dwell	banòn	3	banova
	dërmòj	thrash	dermòn	3	dermova
	harròj	forget	harròn	3	harrova
	largòj	separate	largòn	3	largova
	daj	take away	dan	3	dava
	bëzâj	call	bëzân	1b	bëzâjta
	vê	put	vê	1c	vûna
	vîj	come	vjen	1c	erdha
	hŷj	enter	hŷn	1b	hŷna
	lâ	leave	lê	2	lash (!)
	zâ	seize	zê	1c	zûna

Select Paradigms

prs. ind.	sg. 1	sg. 2	sg. 3	pl. 1	pl. 2	pl. 3
I	jam	je	âsht	jemi	jeni	janë
	kam	ke	ka	kemi	keni	kanë
	them	thu	thotë	themi	thoni	thonë
II	prish	prish	prish	prish-im	-ni	-in
	(j)ap	(j)ep	(j)ep	(j)ap-im	(j)ep-ni	(j)ap-in
III	bi	bi	bi	bi-më	-ni	-në
	du	do	do	du-më	do-ni	du-në
	rri	rri	rri	rri-më	-ni	-në
IV	rris	rrit	rrit	rris-im	rrit-ni	rris-in
	flas	flet	flet	flas-im	flit-ni	flas-in
V	punòj	punòn	punòn	punoj-më	puno-ni	punoj-në
	vîj	vjen	vjen	vîj-më	vî-ni	vîj-në
ipf. ind.						
I	ishje	ishje	ishje	i-shim	-shit	-shin
	kishje	kishje	kishje	ki-shim	-shit	-shin
	thoshje	thoshje	tho-shte	-shim	-shit	-shin
II	prish-je	-je	-te	-shim	-shit	-shin
	(j)ep-je	-je	-te	-shim	-shit	-shin
III	bi-je	-je	bi-nte	bi(j)-shim	-shit	-shin
	do-je	-je	do-nte	do-shim	-shit	-shin
	rri-je	-je	-nte	-shim	-shit	-shin
IV	rris-je	-je	-te	rrhit-shim	-shit	-shin
	flis-je	-je	-te	-shim	-shit	-shin
V	puno-je	-je	-nte	-(j)shim	-(j)shit	-(j)shin
	vî-je	-je	-nte	-shim	-shit	-shin

prs. sbj.

	sg. 1	sg. 2	sg. 3	
I	të jemë	të jeshë	të jetë	All plurals = prs. ind. forms except pl. 3 jenë, kenë.
	kemë	keshë	ketë	
	them	thushë	thotë	
II	prish	-ish	-i	
	jap	-ish	-i	
III	bije	bishë	bjerë	
	du	dushë	detë	
	rri	-shë	-nte	

IV	të rris	të -ish	të -i
	flas	-ish	-i
V	punòj	-sh	-ë
	vîj	-shë	vîje

prs. ipv. (sg. 2 only; pl. 2 = prs. ind. except as noted)

I	ji
	ki
	thui
II	prish
	(j)ep
III	bjer (!)
	dui
	rri
IV	rrit
	fol
V	punò
	sg. 2 (e)ja; pl. 2 (e)jani

Aorist

To prs.	sg. 1	sg. 2	sg. 3	pl. 1	pl. 2	pl. 3
jam	qeshë	qe	qe	qe-më	-të	-në
kam	pata	pat-e	-(i)	-ëm	-ët	-ën
them	thashë	the	tha	-më	-të	-në
prish	prish-a	-e	-i	-ëm	-ët	-ën
(j)ap	dhashë	dhe	dha	-më	-të	-në
bi	prû-na	-ne	-(ni)	-më	-të	-në
du	desh-a	-e	desh	-ëm	-ët	-ën
rri	ndêj(t)-a	-e	ndêj(t)	-ëm	-ët	-ën
rris	rrit-a	-e	-i	-ëm	-ët	-ën
flas	fol-a	-e	-i	-ëm	-ët	-ën
punòj	puno-va	-ve	-i	punu-më	-të	-në
vîj	erdh-a	-e	erth	erdh-ëm	-ët	-ën

Optative

jam	qofsha	qofsh	qofte	qofsh-im	-it	-in
kam	paç-a	paç	pastë	paç-im	-it	-in
prish	prish-sha	-sh	-të	-shim	-shit	-shin
rris	rrit-sha	-sh	-të	-shim	-shit	-shin
punòj	punofsh-a	punofsh	punof-te	punof-shim	-shit	-shin

Many other active tenses are formed periphrastically (as in many other modern languages) largely with *kam* 'have' etc., as auxiliary, a few with *do* 'will.' Most passive mood-tense categories paralleling actives belonging to the present system are semi-coalesced periphrastics consisting of a participle + reduced enclitic forms of the verb 'to be', as prs. sg. 1 *dërgo-h-em* 'I was sent', pl. 1 *dërgo-h-emi*, ipf. sg. 1 *dërgo-h-esh*, pl. 1 *dërgo-h-im*. Those paralleling active categories belonging to the aorist system prefix what is now a voice grammeme *u-* (probably from the reflexive pronoun stem IE **su̯e*) to the corresponding active forms, as aor. sg. 1 *u-dërgova*, opt. *u-dërgofsha*. Interestingly, passive imperatives are also formed with this *u-* which may then either follow or precede, as sg. 2 *dërgo-hu*/*u-dërgo*, pl. 2 *dërgo-huni*/*u-dërgoni*.

SELECTED BIBLIOGRAPHY

The following items constitute a budget bibliography designed for the modest purse of the graduate student. The Sammlung Göschen series, published by Walter de Gruyter, Berlin, will be referred to simply as SG, with the year of publication. From these items, and the recent volumes of the UNESCO Linguistic Bibliography to be found in libraries, a detailed bibliography can be assembled.

Krahe, *Indogermanische Sprachwissenschaft.* 2 vols., SG 1963.
Kieckers, *Die Sprachstämme der Erde.* Carl Winter, Heidelberg, 1931.
Kronasser, *Vergleichende Laut- und Formenlehre des Hethitischen.* Carl Winter, Heidelberg, 1956.
Mayrhofer, *Sanskrit Grammatik.* SG, 1964.
Whitney, *Roots, verb forms, and primary derivatives of the Sanskrit language.* Repr. American Oriental Society, New Haven, 1945.
Brandenstein, *Griechische Sprachwissenschaft.* 2 vols., SG 1954.
Kieckers, *Historische lateinische Grammatik.* 3 vols., Huber, München, 1930 ff.
Buck, *A grammar of Oscan and Umbrian.* rev. ed., Ginn and Co., Boston, 1928.
Pokorny, *Altirische Grammatik.* SG, 1969.
Morris-Jones, *A Welsh grammar, historical and comparative.* Clarendon press, Oxford, 1913.
Krahe, *Germanische Sprachwissenschaft.* 3 vols., SG, 1967.
Hempel, *Gotisches Elementarbuch.* Walter de Gruyter, Berlin, 1937.
Meillet, *Esquisse d'une grammaire comparée de l'Arménien classique.* 2d ed., Mekhitharist press, Vienna, 1936.
Krause-Thomas, *Tocharisches Elementarbuch.* vol. I, Carl Winter, Heidelberg, 1960.
Bräuer, *Slavische Sprachwissenschaft.* vol. I, SG 1961 (vol. II to appear).
Leskien, *Litauisches Lesebuch* (includes grammar, old orthography). Carl Winter, Hiedelberg, 1919.